PENNIES FROM EVANS

D. J. EVANS

D J Evans

PENNIES FROM EVANS

OVER 600 MONEY SAVING HINTS, TIPS AND LIFE HACKS FOR LIVING ON A BUDGET

BY
D.J. EVANS

Date of publication: 2015

Cover design and formatting: Nicky P Gardiner & Davina Evans.

Published by Davina Evans

All enquiries: creationnationstore@yahoo.co.uk

First published 2015.

ISBN-13: 978-1515361367
ISBN-10: 1515361365

DEDICATION

This book is dedicated to my wonderful fiancé Nicky who has pushed me to finish this book for the last two years! His butt-kicking finally motivated me to get it done and published.
He has been a font of knowledge when it has come to saving money, and taught me a lot about self-control – although it took me a while to appreciate his efforts! We have had more than our fair share of lean times but always had a laugh throughout them, and I have felt strangely rich despite them…

I would also like to dedicate this book to the memory of my mother (Linda), grandmother (Margaret) and grandfather (Ron); I have always tried my best to make them proud of me – I hope this counts!

CONTENTS

ACKNOWLEDGMENTS

I cannot express enough thanks to my team of work colleagues for their continued support and encouragement: Susan Canham, my wise friend and colleague who always has logical money-saving ideas (apart from when it comes to her dog – that is one spoilt pooch!); Deborah Hayman, my friend, colleague and a mother who has passed me many ideas for bringing up children on a budget; Clare Baxter, my boss and motivator who seems to have boundless energy and enthusiasm; Jenny Packer, a crafting extraordinaire who patiently taught me to knit and shared many fun things to do by using imagination rather than credit cards (I still think sea glass necklaces are pretty!); Del Canham ('Bruv') who has selflessly sacrificed large portions of his newspaper over the years just so Sue could give me a voucher. I also offer my sincere appreciation to all my other colleagues who passed on their own money-saving tips and sometimes coupons!

My completion of this project could not have been accomplished without the support of Catherine & Kim Gardiner too – they have a wealth of knowledge and a seemingly endless supply of creative ways to get things done without breaking the bank – and they are always there to help – nothing is ever too much trouble for them! I thank you!

Finally, to my caring, loving, and supportive fiancé, Nicky Gardiner: my deepest gratitude. Your encouragement and support when times got rough are much appreciated – I really could not have got through some without you. I love you forever.

Introduction

Good work! By purchasing this e-book you have already made the first positive steps towards saving money. "But how can spending money help me save money?" you ask. Well, this book (along with others in this series) will give you hints, tips and invaluable advice to help you make wiser spending choices and save those precious pounds.

Whether you are just looking to save money for a rainy day, looking for ways to get yourself out of debt, looking for work and needing to be more frugal, or are always on a tight budget and would like some help to make life a bit more fun, this e-book will be able to provide proven advice of how to save those pennies – remember the mantra; "Look after the pennies and the pounds will look after themselves".

This is not an exhaustive guide to how to save money, but is the result of a lifetime of experience of gathering information about how to survive on a budget, yet also be able to enjoy life. I will be sharing my own tips, some ideas from friends and family, as well as a compilation of money-saving ideas gathered from hours of trawling newspapers and the internet, to bring everything together in a neat, succinct package for when you need it!

Although the information within this book will give tips on how to save on everyday expenditure, it is no substitute for if you are struggling with debt. There are companies who can help with free advice, such as:
- 'Adviceguide; Self Help from Citizens Advice' (www.adviceguide.org.uk),
- The Citizens Advice Bureau (www.citizensadvice.org.uk),

- The Money Advice Service
  (www.moneyadviceservice.org.uk),
- National Debtline (www.nationaldebtline.co.uk)
  Tel: 0808 808 4000,
- Institute of Credit Management
  (www.icm.org.uk) Tel: 01780 722900,
- Bankruptcy Association (www.theba.org.uk) Tel:
  01524 545019,
- Credit Action (www.creditaction.org.uk),
- Tax Aid - telephone advice and information for
  people who need tax advice but cannot afford an
  accountant (www.taxaid.org.uk) Tel: 0345 120
  3779,
- Debt Advice Foundation
  (www.debtadvicefoundation.org) Tel: 0800 043
  40 50,
- Money Advice Plus Services
  (www.moneyadviceplus.com) Tel:01323 635999,
- Debt Support Trust
  (www.debtsupporttrust.org.uk) Tel: 0800 085
  0226,
- The Insolvency Service
  (www.bis.gov.uk/insolvency) Insolvency
  Enquiries: 0845 602 9848, Redundancy Enquiries:
  0330 331 0020,
- Business Debtline (www.bdl.org.uk) Tel: 0800
  1976 026
- Step Change Debt Charity (www.stepchange.org)
  Tel: 0800 138 1111

Here are also some helpful websites that will be able to help:

- www.debtwatchdog.com – Information and advice on debt.
- www.debtwizard.com
- www.moneyexpert.com – This shows a comparison of a wide range of services and products, credit cards, loans, mortgages and insurance.
- www.moneymatterstome.co.uk – Online financial education site.
- www.moneysavingexpert.co.uk – LOADS of tips on saving money.
- www.moneysupermarket.com - This shows a comparison of a wide range of services and products, credit cards, loans, mortgages and insurance.
- www.piggybankrupt.co.uk – Information and advice about debt.
- www.shelter.org.uk – Shelter also provides information on debt issues.
- www.talkaboutdebt.co.uk – Useful information and resources about how to get out of debt.
- www.thisismoney.co.uk – General advice on money and money-saving tips. Sign up to their newsletter which will bring you all the latest information.

This first book will offer some useful tips for saving money on everyday life, from the weekly food shop to booking holidays…..

We will start with cold, hard money…..

1 __FINDING MONEY AND PIGGY BANKS__

Collect a specific denomination of coin. I personally like collecting £2 coins. When I get a £2 coin, I stick it in one of my piggy banks (I currently have 3 on the go – more of that later) where I forget all about them. When an event or day out is looming, I have a count up of what is in my piggy bank and am usually pleasantly surprised by how much has accumulated. My partner and I were visiting Lego Land once (for free of course – more about that later too!) and when I checked in my £2 jar, I found that I had collected £68! This meant that we didn't have to withdraw any extra money for that day out as it just about covered the two soft drinks we bought in the park! (Just kidding, although it's worth taking a packed lunch for days out like that as those prices can be extortionate).

Check the change in your pocket carefully. I am reading more and more stories about coins from the Royal Mint being issued with some important piece of information missing from them, or only being issued in a limited number, and they are subsequently changing hands for hundreds of pounds sometimes. For example: if you find a

20p coin without a date stamp (there were some issued in 2008 that were dateless) check the going rate on an online auction site – one sold for £100! Also, in 1983 the Royal Mint issued a 2p coin that incorrectly had 'new pence' instead of 'two pence' – one fetched £600 at auction! Also, at time of writing, there is a 50p coin depicting Kew Gardens which is currently selling on eBay for £50+ (of course, the amount you get for the coins depends on if they have been in circulation. The 'mint' uncirculated ones tend to fetch more than the others). I am also currently hoarding a collection of London 2012 Olympic coins – there are 50p coins and the odd £2 depicting the different events. They are not worth anything right now, but in the future, who knows…

Pick up any coins you find and keep them in a separate jar. I once read a story in the paper about a woman who keeps an eagle eye out for money dropped in the street (coins mainly but I think the odd note every now and then), keeps it in a jar and in one year it amounted to hundred of pounds. This inspired me to be more vigilant and although I have never found that much money (I think the most was just over £30) this extra, free, money can then be deposited into a bank or savings account and give a much appreciated boost to the coffers. Places I have found coins include:

- Car Parks – busy car parks can be strewn with discarded coins – be careful though when walking through car parks – keep looking up as there ARE cars driving around them!
- Pavements and kerbs – as you are walking along, keep an eye on where you are going as well as the pavement in front of you and along the kerb-side. When the weather is brighter is the best time to spot a coin that may be glinting on the sun, half hidden under a leaf or whatever.
- Market places after the stalls have gone – usually there are street cleaners making their way around

sweeping up the area. Sometimes you can come across a few dropped coins.

- Taxi Ranks
- Train stations – obviously I am talking about looking on the platforms and in the ticket office area – NEVER venture onto a train track to look for coins.
- Amusement arcades – My partner and I were on a holiday in Blackpool once and spent a day looking around the amusement arcades. That was a super cache of coins found that day! The carpets in those places seem to be very dark in colour so if you drop a coin it is hard to spot it again afterwards, but if you are wandering around, keep an eye out as you may see a few coins on the floor, and also check out those 2p machines – you will inevitably see the odd few coins that have fallen through and are sitting at the bottom of the machine. (DO NOT tilt the machines though to shake loose a pile of coins – this is wrong, probably illegal, and will only serve to get you barred from every amusement arcade in the country!)

People will probably turn their noses up at the very idea of picking up a coin from the street due to it being dirty. Well, this is true, and I do not like the idea of putting a found coin in my pocket or purse (mainly because you need to keep it separate anyway) so I keep a little money bag in my bag and can use that to pick up the coin without it ever touching my hands until I have washed it. To put your minds at rest though, coins that are passed from hand to hand are extremely dirty anyway. They are covered in bacteria and considering what we do with our hands and then go on to touch money before necessarily washing our hands, we are passing those germs and bacteria around to the rest of the population. In America, tests on money also found traces of cocaine! So, as long as we are not carrying these coins around in our mouths, not picking through faeces to get them, trying to have minimal contact with picking them up and maybe even giving the coins found a clean as well, we are not in any more danger than handling coins given to us at that supermarket! Interesting factoid: copper has anti-bacterial properties and is also non-allergenic, therefore, unless encrusted with filth, copper coins are some of the cleanest coins around…. 1p & 2p coins are made from copper-plated steel. 5p, 10p and 5p coins are 75% copper and 25% nickel. 20p coins are 84% copper and 16% nickel. £1 coins are 70% copper, 5.5% nickel and 24.5% zinc. And finally, the £2 coin's outer composition is: 76% copper, 4% nickel and 20% zinc, with the inner composition being: 75% copper and 25% nickel.

I mentioned before that I have 3 piggy banks on the go. The first one collects up my £2 coins. The 2nd one collects the coins that I have found. And the 3rd one is my 'generic' piggy bank. This is the one that I put any odd bits of coins in that tend to over fill my purse – such as 1p, 2p, 5p and 10p pieces. I let this piggy bank fill up, and then at the end of the year, I will have a count up. I then fill up some money bags and deposit the bags into an account of my choice (usually a savings account, as this doesn't get touched and can be left to build up. Psychologically we are less likely to spend the money in an account that contains money we have saved this way as it represents hard work and reward. It is estimated that on average, every family has approximately £50 sitting around in loose change! You can get those little plastic money bags for free from most banks and are helpful to keep a stash of inside your piggy bank (saves trying to hunt them down when you need them!) and they hold the following:

- ○ 1p = £1
- ○ 2p = £1
- ○ 5p = £5
- ○ 10p = £5

- 20p = £10
- 50p = £10
- £1 = £20
- £2 = £20

Banks will not accept mixed coins in a bag. Also, you need to sort the coins out yourself – most banks will not sort out bags of coins for you. Some banks may only accept 5-7 bags in any one day as well, and maybe refuse them altogether during busy periods, so do check first as you don't want to be carting 20x bags of coins to the bank only to be turned away – they're damn heavy! Also, it is worth cashing in your money from your coin jar/ piggy bank regularly as it can begin to lose value if it doesn't keep up with inflation. If it is being paid into a savings account frequently, you can earn a little interest on your cash and get a little extra back.

You can also cash in your coins at various coin bank machines that have popped up in supermarkets recently. They will sort your coins out for you, but they will charge a fee of 7.9% for doing this so you will lose some of your money – for every £1 you feed in, it will take 7.9p, which can add up quite considerably.

D J Evans

Essentials

2 **<u>FOOD</u>**

Food wastage costs the average household £480 per year. It is estimated that 30-50% of food is wasted globally. 18-20 million tonnes of food is wasted annually in the UK (source: This Is Rubbish – www.thisisrubbish.org.uk).

FUN FACT: We throw away more food from our homes than packaging in the UK every year (Source: **Love Food Hate Waste**).

The main culprits in domestic food wastage are: we prepare too much or we don't use it in time. Considering there are 870 million people in the world who are undernourished (source: World Food Programme), these are staggering statistics and need to be brought down – not only to save ourselves money but to stop wastage globally.

In order to stop as much food wastage as possible, I keep a running shopping list on the fridge (using my scrap-pad as outlined in Chapter 16). We add things to it as we are running out and try to stick to it religiously so we don't end up doubling up on groceries – you know, when you think; "do we have chips? I don't think we do", then buy them and realise when you get home that you have 5x bags of chips in the freezer already!

Further to this, before going shopping, I will have a

quick look though the cupboards, fridge and freezer and make a list of what we already have, and then try to think of meal plans for the coming week. It really does not take long to do this and you can even work on the meal planner as you are in the supermarket. You may have enough in to make quite a few meals already and so can really reduce your weekly shopping bill. Also, when you are looking around the supermarket and picking up fresh products, you can prioritise your meal planner by sorting out the weekly meals in the date of what needs eating first.

Carefully check the dates on food before you buy in the supermarket. I have been caught out more times than I care to remember with this. Stores tend to put the items with the soonest expiry date to the front, so if you are doing your weekly shop, try to rummage at the back of the shelf and pick up the best dated item. And remember, you can always freeze something if you don't think you are going to eat it before the 'use by' date. The best tip with bread is to freeze a loaf and just take out the slices you need – bread is one of the biggest culprits where food waste is concerned and we throw away millions of slices EACH DAY. (Source: www.netmums.com).

Swap to the store's own brand products. It's true that some cheaper versions just don't taste the same – for me, it HAS to be Heinz beans – but a lot of research has gone into not just price comparison, but also taste comparison. Of course, taste is subjective, so you will need to do your own taste test and then decide if you agree that Aldi's chocolate digestives taste better than McVities (apparently, they scored 10 out of 10 in blind tests, but I'm not convinced…).

If you have the time, try and carry out a supermarket price comparison on your weekly shopping. A good, constantly updated, one is at www.mysupermarket.co.uk where you can compile a list and the site compares prices at Asda, Tesco, Morrison's, Sainsburys, Waitrose, Aldi, Poundland, Iceland, Ocado, Superdrug and Boots. You can save your list with them and just re-run the search each week. This is a clever tool, but if you do not have the time to sit and do this, most supermarkets price match anyway, and if your comparable shop would have cost less elsewhere, you normally get a voucher with the difference back (to spend on your next shop) or the difference in points on your loyalty card (such as the Morrison's Match and More card). Don't feel you have to be loyal to one store; shop around and buy where it is the best value for money.

Slabs of meat are generally quite expensive. It works out cheaper in the long run if you are able to buy big pieces, then chop them up into portions suitable to your meal needs, and then freeze them. Keep an eye out for special offers on meat – oddly, legs of lamb (one of the more expensive cuts of meat) is sometimes on special offer near Christmas, maybe because everyone is after the turkey – and grab one or two to freeze for later use. It may be a bigger outlay that day, but you will notice the difference when you don't have to buy a joint of meat for the next 3, 4 or 5 roasts!

If you have the space, see if you can buy other items in bulk too, either when you see a special offer in the regular stores, or if you are able to join Makro or Costco (Makro is free to join, unlike Costco which has an annual fee). I tend to buy non-perishable goods or items that have a long life span from these stores, such as: toilet rolls, kitchen rolls, washing up powder and crisps. The last deal I grabbed was a pack of 24 Cushelle toilet rolls for £10.99 (inc VAT) that was on a BOGOF deal – that was 48 toilet rolls for £10.99; that's 23p per roll. An average price in the supermarkets for a pack of 4x Cushelle toilet rolls would be about £1.95, which works out to 49p a roll (25p more a roll), which means you would be spending £12 more by the time you got through 48 rolls normally! It's a fun day out going to Makro and Costco too – not only are you in awe looking at the vast array and sheer volume of produce you can buy in bulk, but they also tend to have free tea/coffee and a lot of test tables set up so you can try food and drink as you walk around (although don't drink if you are driving!) – no need for lunch before going there!

This is probably an obvious tip; don't do your food shopping when hungry – you will end up putting lots of unnecessary cr*p in your trolley if you do, especially when you walk past the bakery aisle – the effect of the smell of freshly baked bread on an empty stomach is disastrous.

Try and be wary of supermarket 'deals'. A very well-known supermarket was featured on Panorama (the BBC investigation programme) in December 2011 offering such erroneous deals as Limes for 30p each or '2 for 80p'! And the other classic deal of '2 for £2' or £1 each! And be aware of shrinkage – this is where a product is still the same price or slightly higher but the company has actually put less in the packaging; a common example of this is the packets of confectionery; you used to get 4 or 5 bars of sweets for £1 or so, now you are lucky to get 3 or 4, and the size of the bars themselves seem to have shrunk…

Save on food wastage by not always believing expiration dates on produce. Don't get me wrong, you should be aware of the dates put on foods – I do not want you eating or drinking something that is two weeks out of date and ending up in hospital with food poisoning, however, you should know that a lot of the dates are based on the manufacturers' suggestion of peak quality, and not necessarily on any safety issues. Back in January 2015, investigative food journalist **Joanna Blythman** published an article in the Mail Online explaining which foods are safe to eat after the 'use by' and 'best before' dates (check out the full article here: http://www.dailymail.co.uk/femail/food/article-2978826/Ten-foods-safely-eat-use-dates-revealed.html).

She advises that salty foods are generally OK as they have been preserved; such as a jar of pickles. Also, highly sugary foods such as honey or jam are usually fine as large levels of sugar also have a preservative effect. If your hard cheese goes mouldy on the exterior, it fine to cut this off and eat the interior – and the same goes with bread. If your eggs are just past their expiration date, they can still be used in baking or hard-boiled. In fact, here is the list of eleven foods (according to the report) that can be consumed after their 'use by' dates:-

1. **Milk**: Pasteurised milk will keep 50 per cent longer if you store it at a lower temperature. Try storing at the back of the fridge rather than the fridge door. If your milk has gone sour, use it to make pancakes.

2. **Eggs**: According to a report by food scientist **Dana Gunders**, eggs can last for three to five weeks. But they have to be kept at a temperature below 5C (41F), as that helps prevent potential growth of Salmonella enteritidis.

3. **Sugary foods**: Anything with a large amount of sugar, such as jams or honeys, are safe to be consumed.

4. **German sauerkraut and Korean kimchi**: Safe as they are foods which have been preserved through salting, curing or drying.

5. **Crisps**: While they may have gone soft, crisps are highly processed and loaded with salt so are safe to be consumed.

6. **Biscuits**: Like crisps, biscuits are also highly processed and thus can be consumed long after their sell-by date. If they taste soft or soggy simply pop them in the oven to get them crunchy again.

7. **Dry pasta**: Dry goods such as uncooked pasta, as long as it is stored in airtight containers, can keep indefinitely.

8. **Bread**: Keep it in the freezer and it will last for ages. Just make sure you cut out the mouldy bits if you spot any.

9. **Canned foods**: Extend the shelf life of canned

products by storing them in a cool and dark area.

10. **Packaged salad**: As long as your salad leaves haven't gone mouldy (wilted and mouldy are very different) simply revive them in ice-cold water

11. **Chocolate**: Chocolate can last a long time but it can often develop a white coating, known as the 'bloom', when it's exposed to the air. This happens because the fat melts and rises to the top.

As I mention in Chapter 15, you will save some money on your weekly grocery shop if you have a money off coupon for that store – keep an eye out on the front of newspapers advertising these, or maybe friends and family could donate them to you if they have the paper but are unlikely to use the coupon.

Try and coordinate your shopping for later in the day – this is when the stores are most likely to be marking down their products that are coming up to their 'sell by' dates. You can get some great deals and still have a few days to use them.

Diversify your cooking range! Read up on different recipes and you can practice using different kinds of rice, pulses, vegetables, beans or pasta – these are nutritional and can cost very little. You can also learn how to use up yesterday's leftovers and turn them into a new and tasty dish, and create new meal ideas by using up what you have in your cupboards already. Go on, make Jamie Oliver proud!

Try and pay for your weekly shopping in cash – it is far too easy to just pay with credit/ debit cards but you lose track of the cost and it can all too soon get out of control. We tend to only spend about £50 per week on the grocery shopping, so, on each pay-day we withdraw £200 and only carry £50 of it in our wallets. That way we know exactly how much we have left to spend, and, if we have had a particularly cheap few weeks, the left over money can either be put into a savings account, or used for a treat (life would be too boring if we didn't have *some* fun – there's always something that we find that we can't live without!).

Eat road kill. This idea for saving money was inspired by a television programme on extreme scrimping. I think I am a bit too squeamish for it myself but this has been done for thousands of years by people in impoverished situations or for pragmatic, ethical or environmental reasons. Quite reasonably, people see road kill as an opportunity to recycle the animal's fur, skin and meat rather than leave it to rot away. Living off the land also teaches you valuable survival skills which will come in handy if you become lost, are part of a survival reality TV show, or for once the zombie apocalypse happens… If you are interested in this area, the best way to start is to speak to others who already forage for road kill and learn from them which animals are the considered the most edible. A list I found on **WikiHow** was this:-

- Badger, hedgehog, otter, rabbit, pheasant, fox, beaver, squirrel, deer (venison), moose, bear, raccoon, opossum (American marsupial which has a naked prehensile tail and hind feet with an opposable thumb), kangaroo, wallaby, possum, rabbit (reptiles can also be eaten, but they might be fairly squashed).
- Rats may carry Weil's disease and are therefore best avoided.
- The grey area is eating cats and dogs; for some, this is too squeamish as these are pets (especially when they have their collars on); but for others, they're not really concerned. On balance, it's probably kindest to pull the pet off the road and to alert the owners to come and collect it.

Whichever country you are in, it is best to check state laws in eating road kill first as it may be illegal or there may be disease issues at that time. Also, wear gloves when handling road kill as the animal may have rabies. There are plenty of online recipes as well, just Google 'roadkill cuisine'. Purists would probably rather use this form of 'fresh' meat than the shrink-wrapped processed meat that can be found in some stores. If this is for you, go for it – just be careful when walking along the roads looking for it, you do not want to end up being road kill yourself!

When you get to the bottom of your sauce jars/ bottles, add a little vinegar and shake; this will give you another serving or two before throwing it away.

Use those plastic zip-lock bags to put in open packets of biscuits, crackers, etc… This helps us as we only have a few at a time, and then when we decide to go back to the half-open packet of crackers four weeks later, they have not gone stale and then have to be thrown away!

If you have a take-away, save the sachets of sauces, packets of salt and wet wipes for another day. When we have quite a few packets of salt, I tend to empty them into my salt dispenser – once, a well-known take-away outlet gave us such a handful, I nearly completely filled up my salt dispenser! This is quite wasteful on their part.

If you wish to eat out on a budget, do some research first. As this is such a competitive market, there will always be 2-for-1 deals, free drinks refills, coupons, loyalty schemes or 'kids eat for free' offers. Sign up for newsletters as they give you a choice of places to dine at, and will always send you special offers when it comes to your birthday (see Chapter 15). Don't be afraid to ask for a doggy bag as well; if you cannot finish your meal, it seems such a waste to let the restaurant throw it away – ask the waitress to bag up the meal and you can always eat it later that night, or the next day in one of your recipes for leftovers. Maybe have a snack before you eat out? This may sound crazy, but, much like the rule about not shopping on an empty stomach, if you have had a small snack before going out for a meal, you may not want to order as much, and then not have to spend as much. Don't feel like you have to tip either; I know we like to leave at least 10% in tips for the service but honestly, if the server was rude, had the raging hump or made you wait hours for a drink, then you are not obligated to tip – why should you if the service was that bad?

If you have signed up to be a mystery shopper (as outlined in Chapter 10) then you may be selected to be a mystery diner as well. This way, you will at least get paid for the cost of the meal and maybe even a tad more – who wouldn't want to be paid to eat?

It is amazing how many free samples of things, including food, you can score online by Googling 'free food'. Lots of companies want your custom and are happy to give out free samples of their ware if it means you will turn out to be a return shopper. Be careful what you sign up for though – it is one thing giving your email & address, but be wary of handing over your bank account details – this would definitely seem like a scam site if the offer was just for a free doughnut!

3 **UTILITIES**

Utility bills are the bane of our lives. The term 'utility bill' covers the request for payment of public services such as gas, electricity, telephone, sewage, internet, cable TV, water and council tax. These occur every month or so but still seem to jump out of the blue to take the last remnants of your monthly pay!

Unfortunately, unless you are exempt in some way, there is not much you can do to avoid paying these bills each month. However, there are a few ways to help reduce the costs a little…

You are very aware of all the price comparison websites. They are being shouted at us from every available media, asking us to compare their gas/ electricity, etc... and save with them. Despite this though, very few people go ahead and compare or switch their suppliers, leading to overpaying by £100s or £1,000s of pounds. In the UK there are several highly recommended comparison sites, such as:

U-Switch (www.uswitch.com)
Compare The Market (www.comparethemarket.com)
Simply Switch (www.simplyswitch.com)
Which? Switch (switch.which.co.uk)

and Go Compare (www.gocompare.com).

At the end of last year, I joined the Cheap Energy Club by Martin Lewis of MoneySavingExpert.com as my tariff with British Gas (for my gas and electric) was due to come to the end of its fixed term and I wanted to shop around. By joining this club, I was able to get a brilliant deal for a year with another supplier (saving £150 for the year) and even got £30 cashback! The Cheap Energy Club is constantly updating and keeping on top of the latest deals and you can set a threshold amount that triggers an email to you if it appears you could save more money with another supplier (I have mine set at £75, so an email will come up if I can save £75 or more a year by switching to another supplier – it is not much of a hassle to do it, but £75 gives me a little more motivation than a saving of £20 a year!). The good thing about using the comparison sites is that the energy company you are switching to will deal with the old company for you – so no awkward phone calls to the supplier, begging to be let go, only to be sweet-talked into paying an even higher tariff!

If you are paying a lot for your phone/ internet/ TV package, it is definitely worth a phone call to your current provider and try to hone your negotiation skills. It really can work by calling up and threatening to leave them if they cannot lower your monthly bill. Customer service is paramount for these companies as it is a very competitive market so they will invariably try to keep your custom, reward your loyalty and give you a much better deal. NOTE: It is worth doing some research on www.uswitch.com first though as they can compare the current top deals – just in case you are asked for some kind of proof that the other provider will most definitely let you have every digital channel known to man, 1000mb of broadband and free calls to anywhere in the world for £9.99 a month…!

It may be worth having a water meter fitted. Essex Water will also let you install a meter for free but swap it back if you are not happy after a year – so you have nothing to lose really.

If you do go for a water meter, you will need to be very aware of your water consumption; little things like having a four-minute shower, or even keeping your old bath water in a bucket and using it to fill up the cistern (yes, this is a real tip given to me by someone!) can help to reduce water wastage. Other (more sane) ideas include:

- Get a water butt to collect rain water for watering your plants
- Put a heavy block in your toilet cistern – this displaces the water in the cistern and uses less to fill it back up again. Just make sure it doesn't get caught up in the working mechanisms of the cistern!
- When peeling vegetables, use a bowl of water to rinse the veggies rather than having a tap running all the time.
- Turn the tap off when brushing your teeth – you waste 6 litres of water a minute by having it running – think of it as watching £1 coins running down the sink.
- Fix any leaks promptly.
- Try not to flush *every* time you use the loo. I heard a good saying once that goes 'let the yellow mellow' – each flush uses seven litres of water so flush wisely.
- Invest in an aerated shower head. These reduce the flow of the water but should not reduce the pressure as air is mixed with the water to produce a steady flow.
- If you have a dishwasher, only turn it on when you have a full load – a lot of modern dishwashers have 'economy' settings which use less water and energy.
- You won't need to pre-rinse in the dishwasher if you pre-scrape the places before putting them in!
- Only use washing machines when you have a full load as well.
- Only fill the kettle with the water you need – this will reduce water wastage and energy use.

- Don't throw away leftover water in glasses or from kettles – use it to feed the plants.
- If you keep the lid on your saucepan whilst boiling, you will not lose so much water to steam, and your vegetable will boil quicker.
- Use a watering can rather than a hosepipe to water garden plants.

You can maximise your radiator output by wrapping tin foil around some cardboard and placing it behind your radiator. The science behind this is that it should reflect the heat back into the room and, hopefully, save a little money on heating bills.

Heat your home using tealights and some clay pots. You will need 4x tealight candles, an old roasting tin, a trivet, a 5" and a 9" clay pot with drainage holes in the bottom. Place the candles in the middle of the roasting tin and put the trivet over the top of this (so it sits 1-2cm or so above the flame. Light the candles. Put the smaller pot (upside down) over the 4x candles, and put a strip of foil over the drainage hole of the smaller pot (this will trap the heat in the smaller pot). Place the bigger pot, upside down, on top of the small pot (this will act as the radiator. The tealights should burn for about an hour or so and is very effective. DO NOT leave naked flames unattended. Also, the tin will get very hot so make sure it sits on a non-flammable surface, and away from any flammable materials.

You can save money on heating your home by also turning off the heating when it is not needed, only heat parts of your home that you are using and ensure that your home is insulated properly so that heat is not escaping out of the home.

If you have a chimney, it may be worth investing in a chimney balloon. They stop cold air from coming down the chimney into the home, and also stop the warmth from escaping up out of it! They can be easily deflated and taken out when you want to use the chimney as well.

Unplug any chargers when not in use. The reason they get so warm is because they are still drawing power even if not plugged into the device they are charging.

Check that your home is in the correct council tax band. You can start by going to www.gov.uk/council-tax-bands. If you find that you are in the incorrect band, you can ask for a reassessment, but this does not guarantee that you will be moved down a band – you could get moved up! Do some research first to see what your home was valued at in 1991 (when council tax was first introduced) compared to what today's value is. You should really also check your neighbours' house values as there may have been some modifications to your property that explains any difference in the banding (extensions, etc…) and they are not likely to be impressed with you if their banding goes up a notch!

If you live alone, you should be able to claim a 25% discount on your council tax bill; known as a single person's discount. This won't be affected if someone under the age of 18 lives with you. Your local authority should be able to give you more information on this.

4 **CLOTHING**

Fashions seem to change daily and keeping up with them would take a huge budget. Magazines are very good at showing catwalk fashions and the high street alternatives, but if you are not interested in being 'bang on trend' then you can find some great deals on clothing by following these tips:-

Upcycle your clothes. This is the trendy art of taking an old, tired piece of clothing and refashioning it into something even better than when it started. It is not a new concept; even during 30's and 40's wartime, people were upcycling doors to make tables and sacks to make dresses. There are some amazing examples of DIY upcycling on Pinterest, and plenty of tutorials online as well as in your local library.

Charity shops/ Boot/ Jumble Sales. These stalls don't just have second-hand goods, you can sometimes find a cache of new or nearly new clothes that people just don't want anymore.

Low-End Retailers. By this I mean those high street stores that are able to make and sell lower priced products. Cheaper does not always mean lower quality and these stores have sales across the year as much as the higher-end stores so you may find an even better bargain. It is a false economy if you buy cheap clothes that fall apart after the first wash so the best thing to do is keep an eye out for the following: if it has a zip, try to ensure it is metal (they last longer). Good quality materials are usually cotton, wool, silk and linen – cheaper materials like polyester blends tend to start 'pilling' after a few washes. An item that comes with spare buttons is a good sign that the manufacturer believes it will be around for a while, and will only need minor repairs. Check the thread used on the material – if it is too flimsy it may pull apart – also check the stitching to make sure it is not unravelling or loose. Make sure the seams are straight – they shouldn't be crooked or coming apart, and again the stitching should be good. Most budget clothing companies will try and save money by scrimping on material; check that the symmetric parts of the item are aligned – you don't want one sleeve shorter than the other.

Classic looks. There are several staples of clothing for men and women that are timeless and will always have a place in your wardrobe:-

MEN

- White T-Shirt
- Jeans
- Black suit
- Black belt
- Collared button shirts (white as a staple)
- Ties
- Trench coat
- Polo
- Black dress shoes
- Sports coat/ blazer
- Khakis/ Chino trousers
- Watch
- Casual shoes (trainers, boat shoes, loafers)

WOMEN

- o Trench coat
- o Dark wash boot-cut jeans
- o Pencil skirt
- o Tailored button blouse
- o Black jacket/ blazer
- o Black suit
- o Satchel in neutral colour
- o Little black dress/ wrap dress
- o V-neck white T-shirt
- o Crewneck jumper/ sweater
- o Black dress shoes/ pumps
- o Leather jacket
- o Watch (even if you use your phone for the time, it looks very smart with a suit)

You may notice some similarities between the men's and women's list – some looks are timeless regardless of gender. Once you have the basics, you can dress up or down depending on the occasion.

Shop out of season. You may get a great deal on that trench coat if you buy it in July…

Shop online. Much like any purchase, if you find the perfect item, have tried it on and it fits like a dream, have a look online to see if you can get it cheaper elsewhere. When buying for children, you can even bulk buy in one listing for the child, then when they have grown out of the clothes, sell them on again in another bulk listing. Just make sure that the sizes translate correctly on the website.

Clothing exchange. Also known as swishing (from the dictionary definition "to rustle", therefore: rustling clothes from friends). Quite a few 'swap shops' have opened up in London where you can take your old clothes and shoes and swap them – these are not usually interested in supermarket-brand clothes though, they want your old Armani and Gucci cast-offs only! For more down-to-earth fashion, keep an eye out for local community clothes-swap events, or, even better, host one yourself with your friends and family.

Plan ahead for special occasions. If you have some notice for a big event, use this time wisely when planning what you are going to wear. There have been many times when I have left things to the last minute and then spent more than I wanted to due to panicking and being in desperation.

Try to avoid 'dry clean only'. Unless the item is something you rarely ever use, you can end up spending hundreds of pounds over time in dry cleaning bills.

Sell what you don't wear. You can generate money for your new clothes by selling off old ones. A good rule of thumb is: if you haven't worn it in a year, chances are you probably aren't going to wear it again. Be ruthless.

If you are petit, buy in the children's section. If you are of the smaller stature, you can save money by buying children's sized clothes. This is not embarrassing – this is being practical! Even if you don't think it, you are lucky if you are able to do this. This can even apply if you are looking for a generic item like a white T-shirt – have a look in the kids or men's section (the men's section is often cheaper than the women's as well).

5 <u>CLEANING AND HOUSEHOLD TIPS</u>

Cleaning products can be pricey. Getting cleaners in can be pricey. Here is a selection of the best tips to help with cleaning all kinds of things, along with a selection of my favourite household tips:-

When it comes to changing your toothbrush, keep the old one(s) under the sink when you need to scrub in those hard-to-reach areas.

Remove toilet smells by lighting a match and letting it burn for a few seconds.

Keep spiders out of boots and shoes – put stockings over the tops and secure with elastic bands.

Cutting through coarse sandpaper or folder sheets of aluminium foil will keep shears and scissors sharp.

Get rid of marker pen from hard surfaces by spraying with hairspray and then wiping off.

If there are small pieces of broken glass on the floor, press bread on to the area to pick these up.

Clean the bottom of your iron by sprinkling salt on to the ironing board, and then running the iron back and forth.

Get rid of dog and cat hair from clothes and furniture by rubbing with damp rubber gloves.

Clean dirty microwave ovens by adding 4 tablespoons of lemon juice to a cup of water in a microwave-safe bowl. Microwave on full power for 5 minutes. Steam will have condensed within the microwave and you can then just wipe clean with a cloth.

Stainless steel sinks can be brought back to their gleaming sparkly-ness by leaving a sink full of water with two dentures-cleaning tablets mixed in overnight. Use the water to clean the draining board too. You can also remove fingerprints from all stainless steel surfaces by putting some baby oil on to a napkin and wiping away.

Make shower curtains like new again by putting into the washing machine with your normal amount of washing powder/ liquid, a cup of bleach and a cup of white vinegar. You can also add some white towels to the wash, along with some fabric softener to keep the curtain clean. I have also cleaned my shower curtain by putting it in a bucket mixed with water and bleach and leaving for a few hours. I then rinsed it off and hung it back up to drip dry – the wrinkles fell out after a day or so.

Pour boiling water down your drains once a week to try to keep any clogged-up drains at bay. DON'T pour oil down the drains – keep an old bottle that you can pour the oil into instead.

Get rid of mould and mildew from bathrooms by spraying with a mix of bleach and water.

Dissolve limescale from toilet bowls by pouring flat cola into the bowl and leaving it overnight.

You can also get rid of limescale from shower heads by filling a bowl with heated up white vinegar (heated in a saucepan) and placing the shower head in it for an hour. Once done, scrub the shower head with an old toothbrush and then rinse it.

The same mixture can be used when cleaning limescale from taps. This time though, wrap paper towels around the offending area and saturate the towels with the hot vinegar. Again, after an hour, scrub down with the toothbrush and rinse away.

A cream cleaner and sponge is best for washing the bath – don't use scourer pads though as they can scratch up the bath.

Make handmade liquid soap by mixing the odd bits of leftover soap with warm water and glycerine.

Drawing a chalk line around your house will stop ants from coming in.

Get rid of sticky residue from stickers by using eucalyptus oil.

Vacuum mattresses regularly to remove the dead cells and dust mites (also the area surrounding the bed). Another tip is to place your mattress out in the sun – this will kill dust mites as well but can be a bit of a physically challenging task.

Clean your oven easily by scraping out the debris that will come loose with a spatula. Sprinkle a cup of baking soda over the floor of the oven. Pour white vinegar in a squirty bottle and spray all over the baking soda. Mix with fingers if need be to make a paste and ensure every part of the over floor is covered. Leave for twenty minutes. Get a scrubbing pad and start scrubbing in a circular motion – the dirt should come off easily.

Once you have cleaned your oven, keep it clean by lining the bottom with a non-stick oven liner – this can be taken out, wiped down and placed in the dishwasher before using again. Also, clean up any spills straight away, this will stop them becoming dried on and harder to clean.

If you have a marble work surface, buff with car polish – this will reduce the risk of stains.

You can reuse sponges quite a few times in a sanitary way. They are a breeding ground for millions of bacteria so, every night, rinse it out and place it in the microwave for two minutes on high. It will last longer and you will only have to throw it away when it's shredded and smelly!

Clean top to bottom – so when you have cleaned the work surfaces and the crumbs, etc… have fallen to the floor, the floor is the last place to clean.

If you use a Swiffer for hard floors, you don't have to get rid of the cloth every time. I hoover off the fluff and particles that have clung to it and then use again. I only really replace them once a month or so, and then I look around for the cheapest cloths available. You could even use a duster and wash them with your towels to save even more money.

Clean floors by working from the furthest corner to the door – once finished washing or vacuuming, you shouldn't see any footprints.

To remove oil from silk materials, rub cornflour into the area, and then brush off. Cover the area again with more cornflour, leave for a few hours, then shake off and either hand wash or put on a delicate cycle in your washing machine.

Dab clear nail varnish onto the thread ends to stop buttons from becoming loose or undone.

Take a laundry basket and do a sweep of each room picking up items that don't belong there, circle the house and put things away in each room as you enter at the same time.

Clean silver cutlery by lining a bowl with foil (shiny side up), put a mug of soda crystals in the bowl, and fill with hot water. Put in the cutlery and they will shine again in minutes. Remove and rinse off the soda, then dry and buff with a dust cloth.

You can make a candle last longer by putting it in a plastic bag and then placing in the freezer for 24 hours before use.

Stop mirrors steaming up; rub dry soap over it, then rub in with a clean cloth.

When you clean windows, clean inside horizontally and outside vertically – that way you will know which side of the glass any streaks have come from!

If you spill red wine on a carpet, douse with soda water and keep dabbing with paper towels until no colour shows on the towel anymore.

Clean your toaster by using Cream of Tartar. Mix it with a few drops of water, scrub it with a sponge and then wipe clean.

Do you have spare pillow cases? And a ceiling fan? Clean the ceiling fan blades by sliding the pillow over one of the blades and wiping with the top side of the pillow case. This catches all of the dirt in the case.

Get rid of scratches in wooden furniture by mixing half a cup of white vinegar with half a cup of olive oil. Take a rag and start rubbing in – the scratches will disappear!

Make your barbeque grill non-stick by cutting an onion in half and rubbing onto the heated grill (always be careful around hot appliances and naked flames though).

Pour a cup of white vinegar into the bottom of your dishwasher and it will get rid of any cloudiness that has built up on your glassware. Just toss that cup of vinegar on the bottom of the dishwasher, not into any of the slots.

Run hot water before starting the dishwasher: Before starting the cycle, turn on the faucet and run until the water is hot to the touch. This means your first dishwasher fill cycle will be hot, instead of cold, until it finally makes its way over from the hot water heater. This is an especially important tip in winter time, as it takes longer for the water to heat up.

Lemons are your friends! They cut though grease and dirt and smell nice. You can put a slice in the bottom of the bin to neutralise odours. Cut up a lemon into chunks and put them in your kettle; fill with water and boil, leave to stand overnight and pour away the next day – rinse thoroughly and you should have a beautiful descaled kettle. Add a squeeze to water when cooking rice to stop it sticking and give a nice flavour. Squeeze some lemon juice in your hair before going in the sun to get some free highlights. Put lemon juice on any fruit or veg that has been sliced to stop it oxidising. Add half a lemon to your dishwasher to freshen it and your dishes. Lemon juice can get ball point pen off clothes. It can be a good skin toner. They can remove rust spots from cutlery (fill a glass and put cutlery in it for half an hour). And you can make lemonade with them!

Spring cleaning is a good idea, but don't forget to clean in the autumn/fall as well. This way, you can clear out any dirt, pollen, dust and other summer allergens before the onset of winter.

Play music while doing the housework. I try to have upbeat music on when cleaning as this helps to motivate me (who doesn't moonwalk to Michael Jackson's 'Beat It' whilst Swiffering?!) and makes the chore more bearable. No one *likes* cleaning – I'm sure even obsessive compulsive cleaners don't *enjoy* it much – but you can damn well try to make the time doing it more enjoyable, have a dance and burn some calories at the same time.

If you are about to throw out old, worn out clothes, STOP! Cut up old pairs of Y-fronts, socks and T-shirts and stick them in your cleaning cupboard to be re-used as dusters.

Sweep the outside of your house and add doormats. This will stop at least some of the dirt from making its way inside. Make people remove their shoes at the door as well. Shake and vacuum doormats when you vacuum the rest of the house.

Get rid of burnt-on stains from pans by pouring enough cola (any stores own brand is fine) to cover the stain, boil, stir, remove from heat and pour away. The residue should pour away as well, and then you can rinse off and dry.

EXTRA EXPENSES

6 **CHILDREN**

The average cost of raising a child in the UK from birth to the age of twenty-one is almost £230,000 (source: Liverpool Victoria Insurance, January 2015) and this has increased by 63% since 2003 since this survey first began. That works out to £10,952 per year (although the first four years are shown to be the most expensive)! According to the report by LV, almost two thirds of this total expense is associated with childcare costs and education (such as uniforms, school trips, etc...). The idea of one parent staying at home whilst the other goes out to work is fast becoming a thing of the past with one in five mothers needing to go back to work sooner than expected for financial reasons.

With this in mind, even though I cannot guarantee that if you follow the following money saving tips you will not have to go back to work, you may be able to make the path a slightly less bumpy one...

BREASTFEEDING:
Babies can start eating solids at the age of 4-6 months old, when they have doubled their birth weight. If you use baby milk formula at a cost of about £10 a week for the

first six months before you wean off, this will cost in the region of £240. As well as the financial saving, the World Health Organisation recommends breastfeeding as the best choice for babies. The formula will provide the nutrients that the child needs to grow and thrive, but breast milk (if it is possible for the mother to breastfeed) is proven to provide so much more; it helps to prevent allergies, protect against many chronic conditions and can help defend against infections. Breastfeeding is free to do; you won't need to buy bottles, teats, sterilising equipment, etc… (unless you wish to express the milk), and, as breastfed babies are statistically less likely to get ill, you will spend less time at the GP or getting expensive prescriptions. Plus, as an added bonus, breastfeeding burns calories for mum (breastfeeding mums need an extra 500 calories a day) as well as lowering blood pressure and the risk of diabetes and cardiovascular disease. Studies have also shown that breastfeeding can lower the risk of breast, ovarian and uterine cancer. Something to seriously consider if you are thinking of having a baby…

BABY FOOD:

You do not have to feed your baby shop-bought processed baby food; you can make your own by processing natural foods (this also eliminates the need for added sugars, salts and preservatives). From the age of 6-8 months, you can start introducing solids foods at the 'stage one' level (thin, runny, highly pureed and strained). Experts recommend introducing easily digestible foods such as butternut or winter squash, sweet potato, green beans, peas, carrots, apple, avocado, banana, pear, mango, papaya, peaches, rice, barley and oatmeal.

At the age of 8-10 months you can move up to 'stage two' foods (this will have a more thick and textured consistency) and start to introduce other foods such as: meats, lentils, pasta, blueberries and dairy (be sure to fully cook meats and egg yolks first). These foods are still at the lower end of the allergy scale but introduce a more fibrous, acidic and protein-rich element to your child's diet.

10-12 month olds can move up to 'stage three' foods. This is when you can move up to a slightly thicker consistency of food, with even more texture and small chunks to encourage chewing. Foods to introduce now would be: beetroot, salmon, lamb and spicy foods (although not too often!).

12 months+ will be when you move to 'stage four' and introduce solid foods (or finger foods). Paediatricians recommend not introducing whole cow's milk or honey until after 12 months' old though.

The only downside is having to spend so much time preparing the foods, but, if you prepare a big batch, you can store it in the following ways: in an ice cube tray in the freezer (each cube of food = 1 ounce) or in the refrigerator (for up to 48 hours).

So, by now your baby is a whole year old, and you should have been able to save quite a bit of money by pureeing the foods that you would normally buy for yourself anyway. If you were feeding your baby shop-bought jars of food (approximately 65p each jar) up to the age of 12 months, it would have cost in the region of £280. Add to that a years' worth of formula milk and that brings a total of about £550. These are conservative calculations, but, you get the point…

BENEFITS:

In the UK, you can claim several benefits if you have a child; there are Child Tax Credits and/ or Working Tax Credits and Child Benefit. It is worth making sure you put your claim in as soon as possible to ensure that your claim is sorted out in good time. For more help with this, talk to your local Citizens Advice Bureau or check out www.gov.uk/tax-credits-if-you-have-baby

Other benefits for when you are pregnant or have a very young child are: Healthy Start Vouchers (www.healthystart.nhs.uk), these are vouchers issued each week to be used to buy milk, fruit and vegetables, formula and vitamins. These vouchers are worth about £3.10 each week.

There is also the Sure Start Maternity Grant which is a one-off payment of £500 to help with the cost of your first baby (certain criteria have to be met in order to qualify). For more information, check out: www.gov.uk/sure-start-maternity-grant/eligibility.

In the UK, if you have completed a Maternity Exemption Form (FW8), you will be entitled to free prescriptions and NHS dental treatment for the duration of your pregnancy up to the first twelve months after the baby is born.

Once your child is at school, if you are on a low income, they may also be entitled to free school meals and school uniform costs. Have a look here: www.nidirect.gov.uk/nutrition-and-school-lunches.

Also, as mentioned in Chapter 13, make sure to sign up for as many baby clubs as possible. Companies such as Boots, Mothercare, Asda, Early Learning Centre and many of the top supermarkets have great offers on baby & children's goods.

NAPPIES/ CLOTHING:

Babies grow very quickly. In the first six months alone, they can grow 1.5cm to 2.5cm a month, and gain 140-200 grams in weight each week. Thus, they tend to grow out of clothes very quickly so it can be a very costly business.

You will need to check/ change your baby's nappy every 2-3 hours so expect to get through 8-10 nappies a day.

Using reusable nappies is the best way to save money (and is more environmentally friendly), especially if you intend to have more than one child as they can be handed down to the next baby. Modern reusable nappies are a lot better than the old terry-towelling types held in place with a safety pin! In Mothercare, for example, they have a set that will see you through from birth to potty training for £160; this includes the nappies, laundry bags, nappy covers, baby wipes and a nappy bucket. This is very cost effective as a child will typically be using nappies for approximately two-and-a-half years. If you were to use disposable nappies, the total cost (including disposable baby wipes) is estimated to be in the region of £1,500. Seeing how many nappies you will need each day, it is worth ensuring you have a good stock of clean dry nappies, or wash a load every day and dry in a tumble dryer or you will soon run out! Always carry out a price comparison before you commit to buying though.

If you are interested in the idea of reusable nappies but don't want to spend out £100's of pounds, there is a website called Baby Kind that offers nappy trial kits, and if this is not for you, you can claim back up to 70% of the cost back (www.babykind.co.uk/nappytrial.htm#hire).

Don't forget, you buy second-hand reusable nappies. A good place to start would be www.usednappies.co.uk/

If you do wish to use disposable nappies, it would be more cost effective if you buy in bulk. Be aware how quickly your baby will grow though and will need different sizes so it may not be best to buy a year's worth of 'newborn' size – unless you can sell them on. Also, if you have signed up for all the available baby clubs as explained above, you may have a little stash of freebies to give you a head start.

You can save money on baby/ children's clothes by using hand-me-downs from family, friends and colleagues. You can also pay-it-forward by donating your old baby clothes to others as well.

Buy second-hand clothes – unless you are a label shopper and must have this season's trends for your little bundle of joy, your child will not know the difference (much like the section on clothes for your pet!) and will have grown out of them within a month or so anyway.

You can get job lot bundles on eBay, and even check out boot sales and thrift stores.

You do not need to buy shoes for your baby! It seems crazy buying an expensive pair of Nike trainers for a six-month-old, not to mention the fact that the child's feet have not finished developing yet! Even when they are learning to walk, the muscles and ligaments are still developing and strengthening the foot's arch; if you put too-stiff shoes on the child, this can actually hamper their development, stop the 'feedback' that they get from the ground, and cause them to lose their balance and fall over more. Save your money on shoes until the child is ready to walk outside – shoes are meant to protect the feet after all, so they don't really need them indoors – a cute pair of socks will suffice in the meantime.

Do get your child's feel measured correctly though. You can save money on shoes but getting a well-made pair can last longer in the long run.

EATING OUT:

Many restaurants offer 'kids eat free' deals – do a quick online search or look in local newspapers for these offers before you go out.

Collect those coupons! Always keep on the lookout for special offer coupons, or ask friends, family or colleagues to give you any they find. Also, sign up for any loyalty schemes for your favourite restaurants – they will almost always send out special offers for birthdays, Easter, Christmas, etc…

Skip dessert. You can always have this at home.

Don't buy expensive carbonated sugary drinks – go for water. This is usually free and better for your child's teeth.

Ensure that your children realise that eating out is a treat, not the norm. This will make it special family time and can be incorporated into other fun events such as cinema, bowling, etc… and limited to once a month or fortnight.

DAYS OUT & TRAVEL:

Again, do your research before booking days out – many places will offer free children's tickets and free travel for children under 5 on public transport.

Take a packed lunch and make sure your child has had breakfast before a big day out; kids may be easily attracted by the bright colours of sweet and drink cartons, but don't give in and pay extortionate prices when you have your own lunch and treats.

Entertain your children at home. You can have a great day/ evening at home by playing board games, baking, having a movie night, camping out in the lounge or arranging a treasure hunt!

MISCELLANEOUS:

Save money on hairdressers by letting your child's hair grow for several more months than usual. Better still, ask a skilled family or friend to cut their hair, or learn how to do it yourself.

Sell unwanted clothes and toys. You can then save the money or put it towards other costs.

Spread out present buying throughout the year; grab the items you need when they are on special offer.

Apply for a Blue Peter badge for your child. You/ they will need to write in explaining any achievements or something they have created. Once they have their badge, they can get into hundreds of attractions for free or for a hugely discounted price. This is a good way to help your child learn how good it feels to achieve something themselves by putting in a little bit of effort.

Don't just give pocket money – make them earn it. Get your children into the habit of helping out with household chores. This will help you out and teach them valuable responsibility lessons. And don't be afraid to not give them their pocket money if they do not do their specified chores. You don't get paid if you don't do your work after all, why should children be any different!

If you/ they can, walk to and from school! I see so many kids using buses or being chauffeur driven to school when they only live a few minutes away. This is a waste of money and fuel. Not to mention a lack of exercise for the child. I used to love walking to school and meeting up with my mates on the way; this is an important part of the day for kids to bond with their friends outside of school. Just make sure that your child is safe and gets home when you are expecting them!

You may be able to save money on expensive toys by letting the grandparents buy them!

A good tip for toys as well is to give your child an Argos catalogue and tell them to circle the toys they really like. Once they have done this, they then have to choose just one or two and this is their final decision for birthday or Christmas. This make them think really carefully about what it is they truly want/ need and maybe appreciate it a little more.

Try Geocaching. This is a real-world, outdoor treasure hunting game using GPS-enabled devices. Participants navigate to a specific set of GPS coordinates and then attempt to find the geocache (container) hidden at that location and is a great day out for families. You can sign up at www.geocaching.com/, find local hidden treasure pots, and replace anything that you take with something of equal or greater value.

7 **PETS**

Having a pet can cost an average of £10,000 per year. And while we would buy anything for our beloved cat, dog, rabbit, hamster or bird, there *are* ways of cutting back on some of the costs (or at least cutting back to save up for that uber-cute Darth Vader costume for your Pug!). Remember, a pet can live for as long as 15 to 20 years so think carefully before you commit and buy any pet. RESEARCH: you can find a wealth of information online about your chosen intended pet, and there are always books available for free at the library. ALSO: check if any of your family members have allergies, as animals can trigger new allergies or make existing allergies worse.

Firstly, if the family is starting to swap top-name branded foods, why not start doing the same for your pet? Many of the store's own brands use exactly the same ingredients as the big names, so, start doing the comparison test and see how your pet gets on with the cheaper versions.

You can save money on energy bills by not going over the top when it comes to your pets' comfort. Most animals are amazingly adaptive to changes in temperature; they can pant when it's hot (they don't produce sweat like humans) and usually have fur so when it's cold you do not need to worry about leaving a fan or the heating on when you are out. Unless your pet starts sleeping under your duvet with you, they really don't notice slight temperature changes – a fluctuation of up to 10°F is fine for your furry friend.

In the same vein, you don't need to leave lights on for your pets; they can see perfectly well in the dark. You also do not need to leave the TV or radio on – you may feel this provides comfort for the animal, but this may actually stop your pet from napping when they need to and cause confusion.

I have read that some pet owners leave taps running when they are out so that their precious pet has its' own personal fountain of fresh water for whenever they need a drink! I don't think I even need to put into words how this is wrong on *so* many levels; not only is this a waste of precious resources, but the cost would be extortionate. You must ensure your pet has access to fresh water at all times, but in a bowl will be fine.

It is worth signing up for pet stores' loyalty card as well. Pets At Home have one called VIP Club. Much like the supermarkets' loyalty cards, you swipe when you shop, get a periodic magazine, get treats for your pet near their birthday, discounts on grooming and microchipping, free health checks at their in store vets, targeted vouchers sent in the post and 10% just for signing up.

Again, when you are looking out for online coupons for the rest of the family, keep an eye out for special offers for pets too –especially the freebies of treats.

You can keep old blankets or towels to use for bedding for cats and dogs.

Save money on pet toys by checking out thrift stores, pound shops and even making your own out of old socks and T-shirts (tennis-ball-in-sock toy is a tried and tested favourite).

Pet insurance can be a very costly but mandatory requirement for your pet. Before you commit to one particular insurer, why not use a price comparison site like www.comparethemarket.com (also, if they end up showing the best deals and you buy through them, you will also currently get 2-for-1 cinema tickets, every Tuesday or Wednesday for a whole year). As an example, I asked for a basic quote for a 1-year-old pug that had been microchipped but not yet spayed or neutered; the best quote came back for £36.60 (annual fee) which covered accident only (cover for vet fees for any unexpected injury) and an excess of £99. The cover was quite good as it included £2,500 per qualifying accident up to a maximum of £15,000. So, if you are looking to just cover the basics (ie: there is no pre-existing medical condition, such as diabetes), this should do it.

Again, as advised in Chapter 2 about human food, you could bulk buy your pets' food (and even non-consumables such as bedding for the hutch) as well. Just ensure that the dates are good before you start stockpiling.

A small pet may be the best start for you if you have a child that would like their first pet or if you are not able to commit the time, finances or space to, say, a dog or a horse! This may not work out very cost effective though; my hamster was only tiny but the cage and all the peripherals nearly took up the entire flat! He was a spoilt little thing…

Costs can soar if your pet has medical issues and needs ongoing medications. You can, however, save money by having your prescriptions filled online at a reputable online pharmacy, for example: www.chemistdirect.co.uk/pets.

You *don't* have to accessorize your pet! They look funny and cool dressed up in their coats and living in their custom-built bunk beds with their funky wardrobes next to it, but, really, it *is* an animal and your dog really won't hold it against you if you do not buy them this season's must-have hot-pants from Urban Pup! Live within your means people – if you can't afford it for you, the hamster doesn't really need it either!

Remember as well, there are a lot of animals out there that need a loving home. In 2010, a Panorama documentary reported that a third of all dogs taken in by Battersea Dogs and Cats Home had to be put down. That was over 2,800 dogs. In the UK, animal charities such as the RSPCA claim to never euthanase a healthy animal, but in a lot of cases this does happen if they are unable to rehome them. If you can adopt an animal, you will be saving a life, freeing up valuable space in the animal shelters and even helping to put a stop to 'puppy mills' or 'backstreet breeding' which are factory-style breeding facilities who put profit above animal welfare. If you adopt, you can be sure that the animal is healthy, it is cheaper than buying privately, and they come ready vaccinated, neutered and microchipped – some even provide free insurance for a set period – all for a small fee.

REMEMBER: The most valuable thing you can give your pet is your love and attention. Expensive toys are nothing if your pet has no physical or emotional stimulation.

DOGS:

If you don't like the idea of leaving your pet in a kennel, or you are looking to get a pet but want to 'try before you buy' there is a website called www.borrowmydoggy.com which could be the answer for you. It started up in 2012 and seems to have built up a trusted community of thousands of members across UK and Ireland. You don't pay each other for looking after the dogs; there is just an annual fee for membership.

Firstly you need to sign up and give as much information as possible, including what experience (if any) you have with dogs, and which breeds. If you are looking to be the borrower, you need to put in your availability, what you would be doing with any dog that you borrow (ie: what are the amenities where you live) and why you wish to borrow a dog. If you are the owner you will need to complete as much info about your dog as possible, such as their temperament, favourite activities and if there is more than one.

Once you have sorted out your profile (for free) you can start looking for matches. You can add specific dogs to your list of favourites, download their app to keep up with any new potential matches and receive weekly newsletters.

Once borrowers are verified, there is an annual fee of £9.99. This covers such things like: third party liability insurance, contact to their VetLine when you have a dog, and messaging the other owners.

Once owners are verified, there is an annual fee of £44.99. This covers such things like: third party liability insurance, contact to their VetLine for your dog, and messaging unlimited local borrowers.

They like the dog, owner and borrower to meet up several times before the borrower looks after the dog alone – this to ensure that both are comfortable in each other's company.

It's cheaper to feed a small dog than a large one, and they are more easily transportable by carrying.

Make your own doggie treats. This can be cheaper than buying them and you know exactly what has gone into them and ensure they are nutritious, healthy and without additives. There are numerous recipes on the internet for this, but you can find a list of 12 cool ideas here: www.brit.co/homemade-dog-treats/.

Whether you make or buy doggie treat biscuits, make them last longer by breaking them in half. This will save money and also be less calorific for your pooch.

Save money on dog grooming by doing it yourself and starting from when the dog is young – they then become used to it as it is part of their routine. TIP: brush out any tangles before you put your dog in the bath, it is less painful for them and you!

You can save money on vets' bills by ensuring your dog

gets enough exercise and you don't overfeed them. Obesity in dogs can lead to diabetes and arthritis which are long-term conditions with expensive ongoing prescription bills.

You can also save money on trips to the vets if you dog-proof your home so they cannot injure themselves on: glass, pills, wires (biting them or getting entwined in them), certain plants (lilies, marijuana – although illegal anyway, tulip/narcissus bulbs, azalea/rhododendron, cyclamen, chrysanthemums, Ivy, crocus and some others), candles (fire hazard), toiletries, shredders (inquisitive dogs like to lick and climb on things like this), toilet seats (they can fall in and drown or poison themselves by drinking toilet cleaners), open windows & doors, gardens that have not been properly fenced to stop the dog from getting out into the road, certain foods (chicken bones, raisons, chocolate), cleaning products and 'stringy items' (string, rubber bands, dental floss, wool or thread).

Choosing a mongrel can be cheaper to ensure than a pedigree breed. This is due to the fact that they have fewer health problems as they have not been interbred.

Puppy/ dog training classes are always a good idea, but you can also research training guides online or in the library – this can be more relevant too as you may need to address only certain issues.

Shop around for poo bags as they can be cheaper in supermarkets than in pet stores. Aldi sometimes stock a pack of 200 or 300 for 99p. My colleague loves them (not for personal use, but for her dog!) as they are strong and have a nice smell. Alternatively, nappy sacks can be used, and even stockpile those plastic bags that you use for loose vegetables.

CATS:

Kittens and cats, unlike dogs, are very good at making their own entertainment. I think they are a bit more self-sufficient, so you don't really need loads of toys for them;

they are happy playing with bits of scrunched up newspaper and shoelaces, however, you can make your own inexpensive cat scratching post by wrapping sisal rope around a log or tree limb. Just ensure that whatever you use is sturdy and won't fall on your pet.

Cut down on treats. Your cat does not really need them. They don't tend to run around as much as dogs, opting instead for a short burst of energy and then a lie-down! Also, if your cat is an outdoors cat, try to come to terms with the fact that they probably hang around a few households who may feed them, as well as catching the odd bird or mouse instinctively. Keep an eye on their weight and cut back accordingly.

Make your own cat litter. Line a tray with newspaper, then fill with shredded paper and/ or sand.

Instead of buying plastic feeding bowls, use a saucer or tea plate. Cats prefer flat serving plates for their food as it stops their whiskers getting caught on the sides of those deep bowls (I think they are designed more for the human convenience of not having to wipe spilt food off the floor if it's in a deep bowl).

RABBITS:

If you live near a farm, see if you can buy hay from them direct – it can cost a lot less than pre-packaged packs of hay from the pet stores.

See if you can collect vegetable scraps from your local grocery store, restaurant or market. The best kinds of veggies for rabbits are: **DAILY**: leaf lettuces, parsley, kale, turnip/ mustard greens. **OCCASIONAL**: sliced apple and banana, hulled sunflower seeds. **LIMITED**: carrots (as they very sweet). **AVOID**: broccoli, cauliflower, cabbage, spinach, brussel sprouts, bread or high carbohydrate foods as they can cause intestinal dysbiosis (condition of the digestive tract - can be fatal).

Rabbits like a project. Keep them entertained and stimulated by providing plain corrugated boxes as they can then chew, bite, move and manipulate them. You could also stuff a toilet roll with hay for a fun treat.

SMALL PETS (HAMSTERS/ GUINEA PIGS, etc..):

You can use shredded paper or toilet roll as nesting material for your pet as long as the paper is unscented and not newspaper as the ink is toxic to them. The best idea is to mix a little shop-bought bedding with the shredded paper as this will at least be a little absorbent and not smell so much.

When I had my hamster, I saved on having to throw away the bowl of sand that he used for pooping in by getting a little sifting scoop tool and then just scooping out the mess and leaving the sand behind for another day (as long as it wasn't wet).

Instead of buying expensive toys from the pet store, you can put toilet roll tubes in the cage of small pets (like hamsters) – they love running through these like tunnels. Most little animals like hamsters and guinea pigs like the relative safety of a cave or tunnel as they are prey animals and instinctively feel a bit too exposed out in the open.

For small pets that need bedding, you can save money by lining the cage with newspaper and put the bedding on top, this way their urine will soak the newspaper and maybe not all of the bedding, so you can change the newspaper lining and maybe re-use the bedding.

FISH:

Fishkeeping is a very complex hobby. You are responsible for keeping a perfect eco-system for your fish and ensuring the water quality is at optimum levels at all times. My fiancé has a tropical fish tank and he could probably open a pharmacy with the sheer amount of water test kits and different medicine bottles he has for every conceivable disease; from Anchor Worms to Hole in the Head (!). Along with having undertaken a fishkeeping course and owning several encyclopedias – he is constantly learning about this hobby and does not really believe in cutting corners when it comes to the happiness and safety of his fish. Having said that, there are a couple of ways you can maybe shave a few pounds off the running costs…

You do not have to replace filter pads more than every six months. Once your tank is established, when you are doing your water changes, you can rinse out the filter pads in a bucket of fish tank water – not under the tap as this will kill off any good bacteria.

Fish food can be expensive. You can save by buying in cheaper stores such as Wilkinson's or QD. A lot of discount stores now have a pet section and you can find some great bargains.

You can feed your fish certain fruit and vegetables. Check which kinds are suitable for your breeds of fish, but you can feed such things as: broccoli, cabbage, lettuce, frozen peas, sweetcorn, squash, lima beans, sweet potato, turnip, carrot, pumpkin, pears, banana, papaya, mango, grapes and apples – check the 'serving suggestions' for each food though as some may be fine frozen, some may need to be blanched and some may be OK to feed raw.

Only having a small tank will have less associated costs.

Investing in an efficient filter will result in lower running costs. It may be best to get one that can filter more water than the tanks capacity.

Keep pipes clean – if they get blocked, this can cost more in electricity as the filter will be struggling to work.

An acrylic tank is a better insulator than glass. Although acrylic can scratch easier and so may not last as long as a glass tank.

A lot of online pages suggest putting rocks, leaves and lumps of rock in your tank that have been found while you are out and about. DO NOT do this. These may have heavy metals and pollutants in them that could kill everything in your tank. Do not just put in any old plastic ornament you have found either. Fish tank ornaments have been specially made – the paints on other things can come off in the tank and poison the fish. Have a look at fishkeeping forums though as there are usually posts for people to sell their old ornaments. You may also be able to pick up bits and pieces from online auction sites; most of the listings will be new and a fraction of the price of the high street pet stores.

BIRDS:

Don't leave your birds near drafty areas. Most pet birds have originated from tropical climates so may feel the cold more. Plugging up drafty areas will help save money on heating bills as well.

You can make inexpensive perches for your bird from various fruit tree branches, such as; apple, pear and orange. You need to ensure these are very well washed in order to get rid of any pollutants or pesticides.

You can save money on veterinary bills if you take your bird to the vet when you first suspect something is wrong with it. This will save on any future massive emergency medical bills if it turns into something more serious.

HORSES:

Keeping horses is an expensive hobby, and one I suspect you would not be starting if you needed to cut back on expenses. If, however, this is your hobby and you are looking for some ways to save some money, there is a brilliant website: www.equine-world.co.uk that is a treasure trove of information about anything you may ever need to know on equine care. There is a plethora of money saving tips for horse owners if you click on the 'Information' tab, then go to 'Horse Care'.

There is also a forum on the Horse and Hound website.

You can make some money by selling manure to local allotments.

This is possibly the best piece of advice I have found

on this subject: mix poo with some water, and then wipe the mixture on fence posts to prevent your horse from biting them – just remember not to lean on them afterwards!

REPTILES:

With the vivariums, specialist UV lights, reflectors, heat lamps and other special equipment needed for these animals, they may be quite an expensive pet when it comes to running an optimum residential area for them. Nevertheless, these can be kept on a schedule, so, if they have unique lighting and heating demands so you can install a timer to automatically turn off the lights and heat lamps – this will help to shave a little off the utility bills.

If you have multiple reptiles, you can save money on heating bills by using stackable tanks so that the heat is distributed between them.

Save money on insects by buying in bulk.

You can make inexpensive tank ornaments by using branches from trees. You need to ensure that any branches are thoroughly cleaned though – and make sure they have not come from a diseased tree or have been sprayed with fertilisers or insecticides. Ensure any sap within the wood is completely dried out (this can take up to four weeks). A list of safe woods you can use can be found here: http://www.reptileforums.co.uk/forums/snake-care-sheets/1032798-treatment-use-branches-snake-habitiat.html.

If you have the space, you could try keep your own colony of live foods, such as mealworms – this will be a cheaper source of food.

Reptile cages need shelters – one or two is optimum – these can be construed from the branches of wood you have procured and dried properly.

You can use newspaper as a cheaper form of substrate for your reptile tank.

You do not need to feed your snake live food. You can

get pre-killed frozen rats, rabbits or mice. This can work out cheaper as you can then buy in bulk, not to mention being able to avoid the icky issue of watching another animal suffer in order to keep yours alive.

8 **MOBILE PHONES**

FUN FACT: As at February 2014, there were almost as many mobile phone subscriptions (6.8 billion) as there are people on this earth (seven billion) – and this happened in just a little over 20 years!

So, we pretty much all have a mobile phone. Whether it is an Android, iPhone, Blackberry, Windows, etc… they are everywhere and keep on coming with ever more sophisticated software. It seems as though as soon as you have had a phone for 6 months, it's now out of date and you simply must have the newest handset. Well, wait! Don't just blindly go out and buy the newest thing before sitting and calculating the cost of this.

As I write this, I have just moved from a contract to a sim-only deal, and my fiancé has a Pay As You Go phone. They all have good points and I will try to give a guide as to what to consider when buying a new phone (with the help of Citizens Advice Bureau as well).

PAY AS YOU GO (PAYG) – This is when you buy your calls/ texts/ data in advance, and top-up either by using a card, voucher, text message, through a cash machine or by debit/ credit card.

PROs:

➢ You only top up when you need to – you are not tied into a monthly contract

➢ You cannot run up expensive bills as you can only use the credit that is on the sim

➢ You don't need a credit check

➢ You can end this service when you like

➢ This can help you save money if you do need to top up every month

➢ These are a good idea for children so they don't run up huge bills for you, and you can still keep in contact with them

➢ Some mobile phone service providers have really good deals (such as 100 minutes, 200mb of data and unlimited texts for £15 per month)

➢ If you stay with the same provider, they can also reward loyalty with extra credit and offers

➢ A nice person may buy you a new handset for Christmas or Birthday so you don't have that as an extra expense

CONs:

➢ You will have to pay full price for a handset upfront

➢ There is less choice of phone models available

➢ Texts and calls per minute may cost more than on a contract

➢ You need to keep topping up

➢ Using 'data' services may be more expensive (such as accessing the internet)

As I said, my fiancé is currently on Pay As You Go. He will credit his phone with £15 most months, but not every month as he does not always use his credit up. So, he lets it build up for a few months, then doesn't top up and uses the credit instead of the deal on his chosen tariff. He is with O2 and when he tops up, he gets a months' worth of free calls to other O2 numbers, unlimited texts and some data allowance too. This suits him as nearly all his friends and family are also on O2. He can text freely, and rarely uses his data allowance as he tends to use Wi-Fi to go online. This is a good deal for Nicky, it is cost effective and he is very happy with O2 and their service. Also, he has received the odd new handset for Christmas so just has to worry about moving his contacts and pictures across to the new handset – and learn how to use a whole new handset!

CONTRACT – This is when you pay a monthly fee for a fixed period of time, generally 12 or 24 months. You tend to get a handset and a monthly allowance of minutes, texts and data.

PROs:

> ➢ The best way to get the most up to date handset available
> ➢ May be the better option if you make a lot of calls per month – say, more than an hour of calls a month
> ➢ You don't have to worry about running out of credit or topping up
> ➢ The deals may be better on a contract than on Pay As You Go
> ➢ You sometimes get free gifts for opting for a contract phone, such as accessories packs, vouchers, tablets or even games consoles
> ➢ You can usually upgrade to a newer handset at the end of your contract

CONs:

> ➢ You may not know if you have gone over your allowance and end up with a larger bill
> ➢ Sometimes, you still have to pay a one-off fee on top of the contract for the most up to date handset
> ➢ You do not have the freedom to switch providers unless you want to 'buy out' of the contract before it expires – this could lead to huge penalties
> ➢ You may not be able to commit to a set monthly amount if you have other financial commitments
> ➢ You will need to go through a credit check – this may be a problem if you have had problems paying bills in the past. Make sure you are on the electoral roll as this can cause problems with you getting credit as well

As I mentioned briefly before, I used to be on a contract with my mobile phone until just recently (when the contract ended). I was initially on Pay As You Go for many years and paid £15 for a tariff with O2 that was the same as my fiancé. Being a bit of a tech-head, I started looking at newer handsets and really liked the look of a particular HTC one. Unfortunately, I could not afford the initial outlay to get the handset and stay on Pay As You Go, so, I left things as they were. A month or so later, I received a call from O2 (nothing unusual, they tend to ring about something or another every few months, just to really, *really* make sure I am absolutely happy with what I have…) and as soon as they started with their predictable sales pitch, I struck first and asked what kind of a deal they would do for me for a contract phone as I had been with them for such a long time. They looked at my usage history and advised that I could get the new HTC handset on a contract with 200 minutes, 150mb of data and unlimited texts for only £11 per month, with no upfront fees. This was a good deal for me as I was topping up every month and it would save me £48 a year. I took the deal and signed up for an 18month contract. I also downloaded the 'My O2' app as it allowed me to keep on top of the minutes and data usage, which is an excellent idea as I was at the brink of going over the data most months... Anyway, last Christmas (5 months before the end of my contract) I received a new handset as a gift, so I put my sim into the new phone and carried on using it. When I received the call about upgrading my handset a few months later, I told them I did not need a new handset as I was very pleased with the one I had, so, O2 said I would be better off on a Sim-Only deal which meant I would only have to pay £9.50 per month, plus I would now get 300 minutes, unlimited texts and 300mb of data – thank you very much O2, I am now saving £66 per year! This brings me neatly on to the next service available...

SIM ONLY DEAL – This is for when you already have the mobile phone handset and just want to pay for the services (calls, texts and data). Although, due to harsh competition out there, some providers will also give you a free handset if you opt for their SIM-only service.

What is a SIM card? It is a mini smart card that fits inside your handset that has its own unique identification number. The SIM (Subscriber Identity Module) is a tiny circuit board that identifies you to the carrier. It stores data such as your phone number and billing information (on older devices, they could also store texts and contacts), and can allow you to move it from one compatible handset to another and carry on using it with the minimum of disruption.

PROs:

> If you already have a handset you are happy to carry on using

> You are not tied into a long contract. Some deals come with as little as one months' notice to cancel

> ➤ You can get a better deal than PAYG and contract and the calls/ texts can be cheaper as the price does not include the cost of a phone
> ➤ You don't have to worry about running out of credit or topping up

CONs:
> ➤ You have to be happy with the handset you have and not want to upgrade all the time.
> ➤ If you switch provider, you may need to have your handset unlocked
> ➤ If you buy a new handset, you need to make sure it is compatible with your particular provider's SIM
> ➤ You will need to go through a credit check – this may be a problem if you have had problems paying bills in the past. Make sure you are on the electoral roll as this can cause problems with you getting credit as well

When it comes to which provider to choose, there are many. The top ones are: O2, Virgin, EE, 3, Vodafone, Mobile by Sainsbury's, giffgaff, Tesco Mobile, BT, Talk Talk, The People's Operator and Talk Mobile. If you are looking for a new mobile deal, it is worth visiting www.uswitch.com as they are always updated to show the best currently available deals.

In our experience, O2 has excellent customer service, and some great perks such as O2 Priority (free app that gives you discounts and free stuff from loads of different companies – for free so far we have had a dictionary & beanie baby toy from W H Smith, sweets from M&S, de-icer and ice scraper from Halfords!), Priority Tickets (we haven't used this yet but it allows you access to purchase tickets for music, sports and comedy events before their general release) and also O2 Rewards which Nicky is signed up to which gives you 10% of your Pay As You Go top ups back every 3 months – that's an extra £18 of credit for him every year!

It is worth checking out if your chosen tariff includes free calls or texts to others on the same network – you may not realise how many of your friends and family might be on the same network and you can keep in touch for less.

I mentioned before that O2 has an app that lets you keep tabs on your calls, texts and data usage. I am sure many of the other providers have the same thing as standard now, but, if not, check your phones settings – usually found under 'usage' – and set your own limit so that your phone will alert you when you are reaching the thresholds of your allowance. I cannot stress how helpful this will be for you as there is nothing worse than finding out you have run up a massive bill when you have worked so hard to budget your monthly outgoings.

Also, when it comes to buying accessories for your phone, don't just buy from the store when you get your phone. Shop around. Online sites like eBay have thousands of phone cases and accessories for a fraction of the price you would pay on the high street.

9 <u>**USE THE LIBRARY**</u>

I could write a whole book just on the virtues on using our public libraries. EVERYONE should use the library, whether it is for reading or other things. The library is the backbone of our society and we don't even realise it. The libraries are constantly under threat of closure due to cuts in public spending, but according to one report, for every £1 spent by the Government, this can generate up to £4.40 in community benefit.

The library is a free community space; it offers not only books for free ('real' books and e-books) but also free use of the internet and computers, use of newspapers, free Wi-Fi, and cheap CDs and DVDs. It also offers word-processing services, printing, photocopying and use of fax machines.

It is free to join the library.

Any book title that you want can be ordered in to your local library. This can be done online or via the real-life librarian that works there. Do be aware though that a new, highly sought after title may be in demand and you may not be able to extend the time that you have it if someone else is waiting for it.

You can also get e-books from the library (perhaps you are reading this on loan from the library?!). People have be-moaned the advent of the e-book and said that it will add to the decline of the library. This is untrue. Just as libraries have never been in competition with booksellers, they are now not in competition with e-booksellers, as libraries do not sell books. People will buy books and they will borrow books. Much the same as people will still listen to the radio, even though we have television now. Sometimes it can be awkward to borrow an e-book from a library as it may not be in the format that matches your device (as at September 2013, UK libraries were unable to offer e-books to Kindle users as the system they use to deliver the e-books, OverDrive, only used the EPUB format which isn't supported on the Kindle), or it has already been checked out by another person, or it is just not available in the library in e-book format yet. Currently, with e-books, the library pays a licence to lend out an e-book, and can then continue lending the title out however many times they wish. This is even more cost-effective to a library than a regular book as it only has, on average a 'loan-life' of 26 times before it falls apart.

Most libraries have now signed up to a system called OverDrive. You can add this software from either the App Store (for iPad or iPhone), Play Store (for Android devices, requires version 1.5 or later), Windows Marketplace (for Windows Phone users), or for your Windows or Mac regular PC, you can download the correct version from: omc.overdrive.com.

Once you have installed the software, you will have just a welcome message on your digital bookshelf. You then need to add your local library. The OverDrive system maintains an extensive database of libraries around the world, so you just need to browse and select your one (you will need to be a member of the library, and have your library card to hand). You can then log into your library's online catalogue and borrow as many eBooks as your library allows in one go!

Once your loan period expires, the book will be rendered unreadable, but, if you finish reading it before this time, get into the habit of 'returning' it so that other members can get their digital hand on it if there is a waiting list…

The cost of renting a CD or DVD for a week is vastly cheaper than buying or downloading it. You can also use the library's online catalogue to search for any CD or DVD title, and then reserve them at your local library for collection! How efficient and convenient is that! If you do not have internet connection at home to do this, you can use a PC for free inside the library to do it. Each library within Britain uses its own online 'catalogue' system (for Essex, it is called ELAN). If you are logged in, you can check your borrowing history, reserve an item, check the status of any items you have requested, extend the loan date of an item already borrowed and sometimes you can even sign up for email reminders when borrowed items are overdue or when items are ready for collection.

The library is very educational for children. The library can be seen by children as a portal to new worlds and possibilities. Using the library will improve you/ your child's reading ability.

Children can easily read 5 books a week – this is not always easily affordable for most families so use the library instead of buying the books! Some libraries also host special activities for children – libraries no longer have to be quiet places!

According to the Office of National Statistics, as at August 2013, four million homes in the UK were still not connected to the internet. Of this number, 59% said they simply did not need to be online, 20% said they lacked the skills needed to get online, and 10% said that they simply could not afford it. Whatever the reason for not having an internet connection at home, you can use the internet for free at the library. This is invaluable for helping children with their homework (a LOT of school homework has to be done on computers nowadays!), also it can help if you are job-hunting as you can apply for jobs, plus update CV's and print them out, as well as make copies using the library's photocopying service... Small businesses are increasingly using libraries to help them grow – they cannot always afford the costs of kitting out their premises with the hardware, software, internet access and all the other peripherals needed. The United Nations has declared that internet access is a human right, and the public libraries uphold that right; having access to the internet means we can take advantage of special offers that are increasingly only available online (for example; price comparison websites) so why should people on low incomes be forced to pay more while the wealthier pay less?

The library is a free community space. They are there for people to use as meeting places and also generally have the daily newspapers for people to sit and relax in a civilised area which is usually rare on the high street!

Some libraries also incorporate information centres and one-stop shops for council services. This is an invaluable resource for all and should be utilised by everyone.

FUN FACTS ABOUT LIBRARIES:

1. The 2nd Saturday of each February is National Libraries day in the UK. This tradition first started in 2012 and was not only aimed at celebrating the library, but also the workers themselves.
2. The first British library was opened in Manchester, England in 1852.
3. Two statues called Patience and Fortitude sit outside the New York Public Library in America.
4. The Library of Congress in the USA is the biggest library in the world with an estimated 745 miles of shelf space.
5. The most stolen book from libraries is reportedly the Guinness Book of Records.
6. Americans go to school, public and academic libraries 3x more often than they go to the movies.
7. 1 in 3 public libraries across the USA has its' own Facebook account!
8. Part of the M6 toll road is built from copies of pulped Mills & Boon novels. 2.5 million books were shredded into a paste and then added to a mixture of asphalt and tarmac to prevent it cracking.
9. There are 288,044,000 visits to public libraries per year in the UK.
10. There are 4,134 public libraries (inc mobile ones) in the UK.

MAKING
MONEY

10 **SELLING ONLINE**

There are a few ways you can make money by selling online. One major advantage of doing this over just putting an advert in a newsagent's window, having a listing in a local paper, or doing a boot sale is that you are reaching a worldwide audience.

I don't mean you have to go to the expense of setting up a whole e-commerce website (although if you have a viable business plan and want to make some money by doing this, then what's stopping you!) as there are some companies already set up and ready to go, waiting for you to list your items for sale with them.

There are the obvious big names such as Gumtree and eBay, but also other auction sites that should not be discounted. It is worth researching how much these companies charge in fees to host your listing on their site, as you do not want to go through the process only to be hit with a large percentage in fees, as well as possibly an initial listing fee.

Always check the T&C's of the website you use to sell your item to make sure it isn't a prohibited item (for example, it is prohibited to sell 'Adult-only' material on eBay, so you cannot use that auction site to sell off your old pornography in order to make a few extra pounds!).

Whilst researching the various online auction sites, I found that www.alternatives-to-ebay.co.uk is a smashing website that lists pretty much all the alternatives out there. And don't forget the online classified ads website such as Freeads as well....

POSTAGE

When selling anything online that requires postage to anywhere, make sure you check the costs on your country's national mailing service websites (for the UK we would normally use Royal Mail or other courier services). When researching postage costs, make sure you weigh up the items carefully INCLUDING any wrapping materials that will be used as those few extra grams of bubble wrap could knock the item up into another price bracket and you do not want to be left out of pocket by not taking into consideration any postage and packaging costs (on top of the costs to list the item in the first place). You can choose to charge people Postage & Packing or offer it as a free service to entice more interest/ bidders so, again, make sure you know of all the costs involved before you sell your item. Also, a word to the wise: if possible, always try to send items using a 'signed for' option. This will save you untold hours of hassle from people stating they did not receive something, and then you being out of pocket as you have to refund someone, even though you suspect they might be telling porky-pies...

Also, if you are charging people postage, keep the costs involved accurate. Don't be a d#*k and charge extortionate P&P just to ramp up the final selling price.

PICTURES

It can be quite time consuming to create a successful listing for something. For starters you have to make sure the photo is good and accurate. People will not be happy if you are showing a rubbish photo, or one that does not even match the item being sold. If you do not have the photography skills to create a professional photo, then you can use 'stock' or generic pictures of the items that you might find online (although you must not steal pictures from other sellers, and be careful if you are using other people's pictures for your own commercial purposes as there are copyright laws to protect people's intellectual property – it is less problematic if you use your own pictures) but, if you do this, make sure that it matches exactly what you are selling. For example, if you are selling a Lego Batman PS3 game, make sure you don't use the picture for 'Lego Batman 2' or the picture for the one on Xbox! As, if you do sell it (people may not pick up that the listing states something different to the picture) and send it off, you will get an irate person complaining about you, demanding a refund and maybe even leaving negative feedback about you which will tarnish your hard-earned reputation. Trust me, a few extra seconds checking that the pictures match will save you hassle in the long-term.

If the item you are selling is not in pristine condition, you must disclose this, ideally showing a picture of the defect. People trust sellers who offer full disclosure and will be more inclined to come back to you as a seller in the future if you have not tried to rip them off by pulling a fast one and selling, say, a comic book that's been half-eaten by the dog but listing it as being in 'Mint Condition'!

Photos are a bit of a nightmare to take, especially if you only have your rubbish little camera-phone to do it on. True, there are free apps and online websites such as Photobucket you can use to make your pictures better, but also try these tips to get the best pictures first time from your phone, tablet or camera:

> ➢ Natural light is best. If you are shooting indoors, then near a window is good. If shooting outside, then early morning or late afternoon is best as you don't get that glaring middle-of-the-day sun

overpowering your picture (although taking pictures outdoors in the UK is hit and miss anyway what with the rain and the lack of sunshine!).

➢ Using a flash is good for large items but might not be best for small items such as jewellery. A good tip is to tape a little piece of white tissue paper over the flash to minimise glare.

➢ You can make your own DIY 'light tent' which will help you to create really professional looking pictures. Just enter 'DIY light tent' into your search engine and a plethora of websites come up with tutorials on how to do this cheaply or for free if you have the materials laying around anyway.

➢ Light backgrounds work best, and try not to have any mirrored or reflective surfaces in the pictures as you may end up starring in the picture too!

➢ Take lots of photos from many angles as you can then choose the best ones and maybe even include a variety of shots in the listing – this will really give people a good idea of what they are getting.

➢ Once you have taken the photos, and finished editing them, keep them in a specific selling folder on your PC. This makes it easier to find them when listing, rather than trying to sift through years of holiday snaps and other pictures.

Another tip: if you are selling something that has been used, make sure you clean it up before you take the picture as the dirt will show up and you won't sell it (not to mention that it will also be more hygienic for the buyer!).

TITLE

You will need to ensure that the title of your listing contains all the necessary information that will bring a potential buyer to you rather than elsewhere. Think of the title as the advertisement for your item, but you do not need to use words like 'wow' or 'look!' as people tend to not use these words when searching for something online. Also, make sure the spelling is correct or you will have dramatically reduced the odds of people finding or buying your item.

LISTING BODY

As I've already said, it is best to have full disclosure when writing the description of your listing. A picture of any imperfections will help and you should also bring attention to this within the main body of the listing.

You also need your description to be interesting, descriptive and specific. I have found that a bold, red title (in a large font) stating exactly what the item is, followed by slightly smaller main description in black, along with bullet points where needed seems to get the job done. You can check out other main retailer's websites to see how they set their descriptions as well as for inspiration.

You must put in as much description as you would want to read if you were the person buying the item yourself. Just having a picture with "This is new" as the description is really not good enough. You are *selling* something, so really sell it and give as much information about the product as possible: what it does, what the colour is, how big it is, whether it's from a home with pets or smokers, what condition it's in, technical specifications (for example, if it's a USB stick, what the storage capacity is: 8gb, 16gb, etc..), weight, etc... You can even put a link in to any other items you might be selling.

Some auction websites offer add-ons to your listing such as a pretty page borders, or adding your listing under many different categories, or having your picture enlarge when a cursor is hovered over it. These are very good, but be aware that they cost extra too and this eats into your final profits.

According to eBay's suggestions page, the following is an example of a good listing for someone selling jeans:

Levi Strauss Women's Medium Red Leather Jacket

Up for sale is this beautiful red leather jacket. This jacket is pre-owned and shows some wear around the cuffs, but is still in great condition- no rips, stains or holes. Kept in a smoke-free environment. Loaded with swagger! Rock this jacket out on the town with your black jeans and moto boots!

Size: Medium
Colour: Burgundy red
Fabric: Leather

As you can see, the listing does not have to be as long as a book – as long as it gives all the salient points then that is fine. The above description paired with some cool pictures should sell itself!

It may be a little time consuming putting together a good listing for selling an item online, but with practice you will become a pro at it, and various websites will let you use the same kinds of templates to just over-type each time, saving you more time.

Also, never fear if you don't sell your item first time around, some websites offer a refund of insertion fees if it doesn't sell until the second time.

As well as selling your old goods online, there are ways of making money just by using the internet, browsing websites, answering questionnaires, earning cashback when you buy from certain sites and even uploading pictures! Here are a few sites and apps that could make you a few extra pounds each month:

FOAP

This app allows anyone with a smartphone to upload their pictures and make some money when someone wants to buy them. And, you can sell the same photograph over and over again.

The app is available from the Apple App Store or Google Play.

You can earn $5 from each photo that is sold.

Once you upload a photo, you need to 'rate' 5 other photos chosen at random in order for your own to be accepted and in turn reviewed/ approved by other members of the community.

In order for your photos to be approved, you need to gain an average of a 2.5 score.

You can only upload pictures via the app on your smartphone or tablet (I have it on my Samsung tablet), but not from your PC.

AMAZON ASSOCIATES

This is good if you have a blog or a website that you would like to earn money from (obviously not if you have a website that sells the items that Amazon also sells – that would be crazy!).

You can earn cash or Amazon credit by adding links and banners on your site, and when someone clicks through to Amazon from your site and makes a transaction, you get 5-10% commission – although this does not work if you try to make a purchase yourself!

FIELD AGENT APP (iPhone only)

This app can net you around £10 a month which is paid via PayPal.

The basic premise is: the company receive a request for specific information; they broadcast this request to all the 'Agents', and you get paid if you provide the information back.

The information requested could be in the form of a

survey, price checks, mystery shopping, reviews, etc... Obviously, the jobs that are more costly (ie: if you have to travel somewhere, or upload photos which use more bandwidth that a text) will earn you more money.

TEXTBROKER

You can earn money to write content for websites, adverts and newsletters. It is free to sign up and you can earn up to €5.00 cents/ word, dependent upon the quality of the work that you submit. Payment is made via PayPal.

In order to be accepted, you will need to submit a test piece of writing; Textbroker grades you on grammar, correct use of punctuation and constructing sentences correctly. It is also a bonus if you can write in other languages too. If you are accepted, depending on what level you are graded as, you should check several times a day for assignments as they go very quickly. If you are graded as three stars or less, there are fewer assignments available.

The great thing about this company is that is does not matter if you are a novice or a seasoned writer; everyone has the opportunity to submit an article. This will then be rated by the editors, and the evaluations given can help you to grow as a writer.

They also have free writing resources to help you to hone your skills and keep on top of ever-changing writing trends.

YOUTUBE

I believe everybody is aware of YouTube? It is possible to make thousands of pounds if your video goes viral (the definition of 'going viral' differs greatly, but is generally accepted as meaning if it hit a million views). Justin Bieber got his start on You Tube (so it can be used for evil too!), Psy released 'Gangnam Style' in 2012 and it got 8 million YouTube hits in two weeks and a video of Susan Boyle performing 'I Dreamed A Dream' from "Les Miserables" on Britain's Got Talent in 2009 was uploaded to YouTube and became the most watched video ever, ensuring that she became a worldwide sensation.

If you like to make videos (not *those* kinds of videos, they're not allowed!) and would like to make money from them on YouTube, there are several ways, including signing up to become a YouTube Partner and being paid to have advertisements on your video – the only problem with this is that you won't make much money unless you do go viral as not many views = not much money.

You are more likely to make money from quality videos themselves. Viewers use YouTube for either entertainment or education. Video blogs are usually popular. We keep tropical fish and a few years ago our Angel Fish laid eggs. We kept a video diary covering everything from moving the eggs to a hatchery tank, to capturing the eggs hatching into baby fry, to feeding them baby brine shrimp with a pipette. I tried to make the videos a bit more interesting by editing them using Windows Live Movie Maker and adding titles, credits, themes, etc… and they seemed very popular.

Video tutorials are also extremely handy. I have used countless video tutorials from YouTube to help me with things as I learn better visually than just by reading manuals. You do need to upload regularly in order to hold your audience's attention and use key words in the title of your video in order to capture new fans whilst they are searching.

Share your video links on as many social media platforms as possible and also interact with the people that comment on your video. You could even make a video based on any comments/ suggestions from your audience!

All the content on the video has to be your own to ensure you are protected by copyright. You are best to not use pop music, movie/ TV or video game footage within the video as this causes problems when it comes to monetising your content, and is in breach of the owners of the music/ visual imagery's own copyright.

ONLINE SURVEYS

You can make some money by subscribing to websites and participating in surveys. If you type 'paid online surveys' into your search engine, literally hundreds of thousands will appear. The trick is to make sure that the ones you choose are legitimate – a good rule of thumb is to steer clear of any companies that ask you to make any upfront payments – you should not be asked to pay for the privilege of completing surveys.

I followed a blog from an author called Chris Guthrie who set out to see if you could really make money from paid surveys – you can check out his progress at this page: entrepreneurboost.com/case-study-intro/. I found this a really interesting case study into the world of paid surveys and he lets you know the best companies to sign up with (such as Cash Crate).

Be prepared to spend a lot of time initially completing a screening survey before being accepted into a particular company. These are quite tedious but they are to ensure that you get matched to surveys that are relevant to you – the less you complete on them, the fewer surveys you will get sent.

If you wish to be paid in cash, check that the website does this. Some companies will pay in high street vouchers or enter you into competitions. If this is not what you want, cross them off the list and move on to the next one.

It is perhaps a wise idea to set up a separate free email account for all the survey invitations to be sent to (such as Hotmail, Yahoo, etc..). This is for a few reasons; firstly, if you have registered with several companies, that is a lot of extra info being sent to your regular inbox (and a lot to sift through). Secondly, you can ensure your privacy – companies may say that they will not sell your information to other companies but it is better to be safe than sorry. Once your details are out there, it's too late! Also, you will most definitely start receiving lots of spam emails from any companies affiliated with the site you have registered with...

You should not need to give reams of personal information to register with a company – the basics should be sufficient, such as name, email address, birth date, gender, and address. DO NOT give your telephone number out as this opens the door for all the telemarketers in the world to start calling you – and they are a nightmare to stop!

If being paid in cash, you will need to give your bank details. You should maybe consider setting up a PayPal account as this is one of the most secure ways to get paid online.

You will not make millions from completing online surveys so veer away from any that say differently! You are probably looking at making about £50 a month (depending how much time you have to dedicate to doing these surveys) but this is better than nothing and you can sit and complete them in front of the TV as they are usually very easy to complete.

FACEBOOK/ GOOGLE+

This is a good way to use social media to sell off anything you no longer want/ need. You can advertise the item(s) to your friends/ family and they can spread this to their extended circles so you can end up having a wide-reaching audience.

Don't just use these platforms to push your unwanted items though as you could end up being blocked by people who get fed up with being bombarded by 'buy this' messages. Remember that these are *social* media sites so you need to adhere to the etiquette of them and be sociable, build friendships, comment politely on others' posts, put thought-provoking posts on yourself, share funny pictures/ videos and only try to sell them your old stuff every now and then!

Using Facebook was very helpful to me recently. You remember those baby Angel fish we bred and put on YouTube? Well, we ended up raising about 40 of them to maturity and our tank was mega full! We approached the local fish shops who basically wanted us to give them away to them (to sell on for approx. £5 each), so, we firstly listed them on Gumtree (obviously for pick-up only or delivery to somewhere local – it doesn't seem right/ logical posting live fish, and at the time I believed that you could not sell livestock on eBay) but had no interest from there. Eventually, we posted on Facebook offering the fish and had loads of interest! This was good in another way as well: we weren't just selling them to strangers. This was important to me as I lovingly raised them from baby fry, fed them from a pipette and watched them develop daily – they were my babies and at least I knew that friends/ family/ acquaintances would offer a good home to them – or else! Additionally, my fiancé has kept tropical fish from a young age and is quite the encyclopaedia when it comes to fish knowledge, so he was also on-hand for anyone wanting any follow-up advice. This was definitely the best way for us to find good homes for our excess fish and make some money as well.

11 <u>SELLING FACE-TO-FACE</u>

When selling your unwanted good face to face, there are several ways that jump out at you: boot sales and jumble sales. There are, however, several other ways as well – here are a few that I have found:

<u>Car Boot Sales</u>

Boot Sales are fun! Sure, they mean having an early start but you finish at about 1-2pm and then have the rest of the day to yourself. Even better, if it's a sunny day, you get to sit in the sun and make some money (not to mention the priceless people-watching you can take part in!). They are mainly held on Sundays with some also on Saturdays and Bank Holiday Mondays.

You can find out where your local Car Boot Sales will be held from either your local newspaper or by conducting a quick check online. Personally, I would check the local papers as some websites may not be updated regularly and the last thing you want to do is turn up to find that the 'biggest boot sale ever' is now the site of a dog-rehoming centre! At least people should not be stupid enough to place an ad in a paper for an event that does not exist anymore...

There are boot sales that run early or slightly later (usually known as 'lazy bones' boot sales). The early ones usually let sellers in at about 6am and are open to the public about an hour later. You pay a small amount for a pitch and then drive through and get shown to your space by one of the marshals they have – a top tip is to arrive quite early as cars start queuing up early in order to get a pitch near to the entrance. A large percentage of people spend the most money in the first 4 rows, so you do not want to end up near the back.

The 'early bird' buyers (or 'boot divers') will try and descend upon you as soon as you open your boot. Try not to be intimidated and keep an eye on your stock as things can go 'missing' at this point whilst you are distracted. Be firm and let people know that whatever they want that you happen to have will be visible soon, so they can either wait or come back.

As well as the goods you want to sell, you will need something to put them on. The best thing is a paste table, along with an old sheet or tarpaulin (in order to spread out items on the floor too), a clothes rail, and maybe a little fold up chair (unless you don't mind standing or sitting on the floor). You could also take some stickers, pens and sellotape if you want to price up all your stock. I also have a little lockable tin to put my money in too, although a bum bag or your regular purse will suffice. Make sure you take plenty of change too. People love paying for a 50p item with a £20 note! So make sure you have quite a few £1 coins, some 50p's and maybe a few notes – failing that, telling people you don't have change for a £50 note will usually prompt them to suddenly find the right money after all!

You are best to load up your car the evening before as, trust me; you will not be fully 'compos mentis' at 4am and will probably wake up and annoy all your neighbours by crashing about in the street and having domestics with your partner! Obviously, if you do load up your car the night before, make sure you have somewhere secure to leave it – it is never a good idea to leave a car out with personal belongings on show (even if they are just smelly old trainers) the cost to replace smashed windows on your car will far outweigh any money the boot sale would have generated. Whilst loading the car, make sure to put the table, sheets, chair, etc.. in last as you will need these first.

Most boot sales operate a 'second hand goods only' rule. Stick to this rule or you could be thrown out. Also, they probably would not take too kindly to your selling things like weapons or guns.

If you are taking battery operated items, take some batteries to show people that it works. Also, people can be wary if you are selling electrical items as they are taking a chance that it works – just promising emphatically that it does with a big smile will not automatically make people believe you. The best thing you can do is make sure it looks presentable (this goes for all your items really) and that the plug is still on it. Just remember, if you sell something and lie to them by saying it works, that person could get home, see it doesn't, then come back and break your legs – best to be honest.

People have differing ideas of what makes a stall look more inviting. Psychologically, the best way is to arrange you stall is to create a kind of semi-circle, such as your table in the middle with items laid out either side. This image seems inviting and lets buyers sweep your stall as a whole rather than letting their eye wander to the next stall. Keep some idea of order to the stall as well – ie: keep items of the same ilk together such as clothes in one place (nicely arranged if possible), and all the books, games, etc... together. Also try and keep the items nicely spaced so that your stall does not look like just a pile of stuff all heaped up in one big pile! Some people find that an acceptable challenge and will dive in looking for treasure, however, most will think 'sod that' and keep on walking.

Take a thermos flask and sandwiches. There will be

food stalls about but they are at inflated prices and the purpose is to make money, not spend it, right? It might also be handy to take some sun cream and a hat, just in case it IS sunny…

Don't do a boot sale alone. Mainly because it is more fun doing it with someone else, you have an extra pair of eyes whilst unloading and who will watch the stall when you need to visit the toilet?! You could either use one car or, if you are doing a boot sale with a friend, have stalls next to each other so you have a bigger selling area as well.

It is worth taking some of those millions of carrier bags you have been hoarding as well – people will ask for a bag and this somehow seems more 'professional'.

Some people arrive early, don't bother setting up their stall, wander around buying up other people's stock, and then re-selling it on their own stall – don't be one of those d#*ks. Be a decent stall-holder and you will likely make friends and be able to go to the same place again without being verbally abused by the regulars!

People will always want to haggle. Make sure you have an idea of the prices you want to charge for each of your items and allow some leeway of about 20% for the person haggling.

Also, if someone buys something quite bulky, it is a nice gesture to allow them the opportunity to leave the item with you until they are finished looking around, or even give them a hand carrying it back to their car.

I always try to stay until nearly the end. Mainly because people are still looking around up until the end and you do not want to miss out on that last potential customer. Note: this doesn't work so well though if you are at the end of a row and everyone else has left from around you – people tend to be put off seeing a wide expanse of field with a single stall at the end with you staring at them – to a lot of them, this does not seem welcoming for some reason…

When it is time to leave, make sure you either take all your rubbish home with you, or dispose of anything in the appropriate way – some places have big oil cans as bins where you can throw your rubbish safely and responsibly, and other places have areas where you can leave unwanted items (things you really don't want to have to take home again and you can't sell online) where the marshals (seemingly gratefully) root through them and sort out the 'trash' from the 'treasure'. Each venue is different though so be prepared to take home any rubbish and recycle or dispose of it in the normal way.

Jumble Sales

Also known as 'bring and buy sales', 'church sales' or 'rummage sales'. They can be found mainly in community centres or church halls. Quite like a boot sale, stall holders will have a miscellaneous range of second-hand goods, sold very cheaply, and sometimes the money raised will be for a charity or special event.

Jumble sales are sometimes community-run and would usually coincide with a local public event (such as a fair or festival). You can find details of any upcoming local jumble sales in your local free newspapers (or their online versions if you do not receive them through your letterbox frequently), sometimes there will be posters up in your community to advertise them (in newsagents, local shops or in schools), local radio stations will promote these events, or you could organise one yourself using these methods of advertising. The following websites will sometimes have information about local jumble or boot sales:

www.gumtree.com
www.carbootjumction.com
www.yelp.co.uk
www.freeads.co.uk.

If you are going to be a stall holder, remember to take lots of carrier bags, a box or bag for your float money, plenty of change, and lunch so that you are not spending the money at the refreshment stall. Make sure to check that the venue will be providing the tables; otherwise you will need to bring your own.

You will need a big selection of items that you are happy to sell for very small prices, ie: a bag of clothes for £3 is a reasonable price at a jumble sale, as is 20p for a book. You could ask friends, family or neighbours for donations of unwanted goods. Also, make sure that the items you are selling are clean and in good condition.

As a tip, you could also take a tape measure with you in case people have questions about trousers or curtain lengths, etc…

Make sure you have plenty of time to set up, and organise your goods into categories such as shoes, clothes, household items, games, books so that it is not too 'jumbly' for people! Again, it may be wise to have another person with you to help out – you cannot have eyes everywhere and you never know when you might need to use the loo!

NOTE ABOUT SELLING FOOD AT BOOT SALES OR JUMBLE SALES:

When selling food to the public as a business, you need to have a certificate from a health inspector. Even if you are just making a batch of cakes to sell at the jumble sale, it is best to call your local authority's environmental health office in order to ensure you are complying with the Food Safety laws. Current legislation says that all food businesses must register their kitchens with their local authority unless they operate on a "casual and limited" basis only (such as cooking foods for a jumble sale once in a blue moon), but, again, check first as inspectors will make spot checks at jumble sales and boot sales.

Yard Sales

These are also known as 'garage sales' and they are one or two day sales you can hold in your own garage or yard.

You can advertise locally using the tips given above, or even use social media to spread the word.

Make a sign or poster to put up at the end of your street to let people know as well – really make it stand out with bright colours and make sure it is legible! You also need to make sure it is weather proof and make sure it tells people the date and time of the sale, plus the location.

As with jumble and boot sales, prepare the goods and the table(s) early, make sure you have carrier bags and plenty of change. It may be wise to have a listed inventory of any bigger ticket items with the prices listed too, in case any price tags mysteriously go missing…

And again, it may be wise to have another person with you to help out – you cannot have eyes everywhere and you never know when you might need to use the loo!

And finally, TAKE DOWN ALL POSTERS once the sale is done. Be a good neighbour and keep your community clean and tidy.

Flea Markets

These are open air or street markets, much like boot sales, where people can sell second-hand goods.

You can hire a pitch and sell your goods in much the same way as a boot sale, and you can find your local flea markets in free local papers, or at www.flea-market-vendor-resources.com.

FUN FACT: The origin of the term 'flea market' dates back to 1917. It references the Parisian *marché aux puces;* so-called
"because there are so many second-
hand articles sold of all kinds that they'rebelieved to gather
 fleas."
[E.S. Dougherty, "In Europe," 1922].

Auction

Local auctions are fun places to take your unwanted goods, offering them up for bids and then selling the item to the highest bidder.

If you have any items that you feel may be worth a bit more than 10p at a boot sale, then you may want to consider taking them to an auction.

Typically, auction houses will want their valuers to assess items before they can be entered into an auction. The valuer can then discuss with you what the item's (or 'lots') estimated value is and if a 'reserve' can be applied (this is a set amount that the lot has to reach before it will sell – the lowest amount you are willing to accept).

Auction houses take commission, and they are always in a win-win situation as they charge commission from both the seller and the buyer so you will need to take this into consideration when selling things at auction. They will charge a commission rate of between 8-20%, and also charge VAT on top of that amount. For example, you sell an item for £100. You then pay commission fees (if this is 20%, that would be £20), then you pay VAT on that amount (£4). This means you are left with £76. Check with the auction house what their vendor commission rates are first, that way you can assess if this is the best route for you.

Newsagents & Noticeboards

Putting an advert on a noticeboard or in a newsagent's window may seem old-fashioned, but it is still a viable and relatively cheap way to advertise your wares. People can advertise anything from unwanted goods, cars, rooms for rent, or, ahem, discreet masseuses!

Newsagents will usually charge a weekly amount of approx. 50p a week to put up a postcard-sized advert in their window. This is a really good way to advertise locally those larger items that would cost too much to post.

Newspaper Advertising

Some newspapers will charge you to put an advert in their paper, but some (like Loot or Freeads) offer free advertising. Check your local paper for any offers too as they may offer a free listing if the item does not sell first time.

The good thing about this is that you can offer the goods at a price you feel is reasonable and people will collect it from you – which is even better if it is a large item, such as a settee or table.

Another positive thing about advertising in a physical medium like a local newspaper, is that you still have that option to just 'clip' the advert to keep for later reading, rather than having to boot up a PC or print off a whole piece of paper (using your own ink and paper), or trawl websites finding the damn ad again.

Advertising locally is also a very positive thing to do as it supports the local community financially (by paying them for a small ad, and local people giving you, another local person, the money for the item), and brings people together. Even though advertising globally online reaches a lot more people, no other medium has the in-depth community coverage that local newspapers offer and reaches a wide demographic of residents; young and old, rich or poor, male and female, and people who may not have access to the internet.

12 **TRADING IN BOOKS/ GAMES/ CDS AND DVDS**

You, like me, probably have cupboards full of computer games or CDs or DVDs (or some of all!) that will just sit there forevermore, destined never to be played or listened to again. You might want to keep hold of them for sentimental reasons, or, you could apply the same pragmatism to them that we are supposed to apply to our clothing: if it's not been used for a few years, then chances are they are unlikely to be used again.

There are a number of ways that you can get rid of these items. You could sell them or you could trade them in. Sometimes you can get a better deal by trading in than by selling, and here are a few ideas for you:-

Trade In Detectives – www.tradeindetectives.com
This is a really handy tool to save you trawling through loads of individual websites. It is a free to use price comparison website where you can type in the name of the game or console you wish to sell or trade in and it will compare the offerings of such companies as: Cex, Amazon, Game Xchange, Game, Asda, Grainger Games, Music Magpie and many others. The results list shows you

the name of the company, a short biography about them, their trade-in price, their cash price, any additional offers (such as whether they offer free postage), and a link to their website or store information. Some retailer's prices are hidden until you register on the site, but this is free to do. This is a really well presented website with a hilarious FAQ page (or 'Frequently Asked (stupid) Questions' page as they call it). There are quite a few annoying advertising banners that pop up, but hey, they ARE a free to use website that needs to make some revenue somehow. Once you have found the best deal for your item, do make sure that you double-check the prices with the retailers themselves as things do change quickly. As an example of prices, I typed in 'Lego Batman The Videogame' on PS3 (which was an old game released in 2008, and this price was in June 2014) and the best trade-in offer was £8 at Cex. Not too shabby for a trade in price.

Cex

I am only starting with this company because they offered me such a good deal on my Lego Batman game! They buy, sell and exchange a range of technology and entertainment products including mobile phones, video games, DVDs and Blu-ray movies, computers, digital electronics, TVs and monitors, and music CDs. They are a multi-national franchise company with stores in the UK, Spain, USA, Ireland, India, Australia, Portugal and Netherlands. You can type in the name of the item, then choose to buy or sell it (it tells you the amount for cash or voucher). Once you have entered all your items (and registered with the site), you can click on your basket and proceed to checkout (there is a separate basket for buying and selling). You are now presented with 5 ways of receiving your money: an In-Store Cex Voucher, Cheque, PayPal, Bank Transfer or Bitcoin (very modern! Although you would need to trade in a lot of items to make one whole bitcoin as the current exchange rate is approximately: 1 bitcoin = £348). It appears to be a freepost address at the moment to send items to sell to Cex, and you can print off a postage label where you would write your Order Number on as well. The website does state that this covers just basic postage costs but is not insured so it is advisable to pay for a trackable/ insured method on top of this to ensure safe arrival. Overall it seems a very quick, easy and convenient way to trade in your old stuff.

Game

The company Game have an online Price Checker where you can look at their current trade-in list for old consoles or games and use this in-store credit against any new purchases. This is good if you want to clear out some games to make way for new games or the latest console. But do check the T&C's carefully and make sure your game/ console is in good, clean and working order. They won't accept multiple copies of the same game, nor will they accept imported copies of games/ consoles. They say they won't be beaten on trade-in prices so do your homework thoroughly against other companies as they say they will beat any other offer by £1 (for in-store trade-in credit).

Amazon Trade-In Programme

Amazon has a Trade-In Programme that is for computer games and books, where you can earn the value in Amazon Gift Cards. It seems quite straight forward where you enter the title of the game or book, click on 'trade' under the correct item, if the total amount come to more than £10 you will be eligible for free postage of the items to Amazon, you then wait to hear back that the item(s) have been verified and accepted, once all is OK, the amount will be deposited to your account. Again, check the 'Product Eligibility' page to ensure that your items are in an acceptable condition.

WARNING – check the feedback first as at the time of writing there were some disgruntled customers. Hopefully any issues will have been ironed out when this goes to press.

Music Magpie

This company will buy your CDs, DVDs, Games, Clothes and Electronics. On the front page you start by choosing which of the above you want to sell (ie: Electronics), then you will be taken to the next page and asked to choose from a series of 3 drop-down menus until you get to your chosen item (ie: for a PS3 160gb you would choose 'Games Console', then 'Sony' then 'PS3 160GB' then click on the + button and it will then ask you to clarify what condition it is in, then give you a quote at the bottom of the screen. Once you are done, you can complete the order and there is a free courier service to send your goods off. The website is a bit hazy as to what happens after this is done and I cannot see how long it takes to get your money afterwards (although the TV advert seems to imply that a stuffed magpie will fly you a cheque back), but, I am sure there are plenty of online forums able to advise if this is a seamless transaction…

Game Xchange

This is an online site that also trades on eBay, Play.com and Amazon.co.uk. You can trade in games and DVDs on there. I again typed in 'Lego Batman PS3 game' and was offered £4.00 for it. The money you make is kept on your account ready to be used against any of their products, or you can choose their 'Get Cash' option where money is transferred to you either by bank transfer, PayPal or cheque. If your trade-in contains four or more items, or is valued over £10, then you can use their FREE Royal Mail Tracked Service (which has a 5kg limit) so it won't even cost you to send anything to them. I have not used their site myself but all looks very well set out, their feedback from their various trading avenues are easy to see, any questions you may have are answered as you go and they have been trading for over 10 years now and have gained a good reputation.

Grainger Games

This is an online and 'bricks-and-mortar' retailer, which currently has 72 stores nationwide. You can trade in or sell your unwanted goods to them. Again, I tried Lego Batman on PS3 and they offered the slightly better deal of £5 for a trade-in, although, I could not see that they offer any free postage service to get the items to them, so would lose a bit by paying to send them the items. I guess you could get around this by taking your trade-in items to one of their stores if they are close by (although at the moment, I cannot see any stores further South than Derby and Nottingham, which would be no good for someone such as myself who is in Essex!). They have been established a while now and seem to be constantly expanding: they started out as a stall within a shopping centre in Newcastle-Upon-Tyne in 1997, and they now have their own cool-looking orange painted Hummer vehicle!

SAVING MONEY

13 **LOYALTY CARDS**

I have mixed thoughts about loyalty cards. There is no doubt that they can be super helpful and points can build up pretty fast if you use that specific store a lot. However, if you collect a loyalty card for each store you visit (either frequently, or not very often) then you end up having to lug about a tonne of plastic and sift through purses, wallets and pockets for the card for that store in a "did I sign up for a card for this store? I'm sure I did but now I can't find it" scenario, with people behind you in the queue rolling their eyes at each other about you.

I now have a purse with wallet compartments, a metal card holder and a zipped pocket at the back of my handbag full of loyalty cards. I had a clear out the other day and sorted my cards out into piles of usefulness. I now keep the cards I use the most in my immediate purse; the ones I use maybe once a month or less in the metal card holder; and the rest in the zipped pocket. I now also try to source a specific card BEFORE I join a queue in a store to avoid embarrassment.

A lot of the stores I have loyalty cards for also send out coupons periodically for use within a certain time. I have a plastic wallet in my handbag that where I keep these (as mentioned in Chapter 15), but I would reiterate again how important it is to keep this tidy as you can end up with hundreds of expired coupons in your bag!

Loyalty cards were introduced by stores to reward loyal customers and keep them coming back into stores. They tend to work by you giving the store your details and they will give you a card with a unique number on. When you purchase something, the sale will generate the given amount of points on to your account. These points accumulate until you have enough to redeem against a desired item. Also, the store will usually collect data about your spending habits and generate offers based on your preferred items (I tend to get lots of offers about chocolate, hmm…) with maybe one or two about things you have never purchased, to try and tempt you in.

According to the Mirror newspaper (8th August 2014) the top 10 loyalty cards were:-

1. Tesco Clubcard – www.tesco.com

Over 68% of the UK population has one. You can accumulate 1 point per £1 spent online, in store or at their petrol stations – and each point is worth 1p worth of vouchers. They also have 'partners' where you can collect points too, such as E.ON, Esso, Nutricentre, Blinkbox and others. Once you reach 150 points, these get converted into vouchers and get sent to you with your Clubcard Statement (every three months). You can 'spend' these vouchers at face value, or have the option to 'boost' them where you can get up to 4x the value of your points and use them with one of Tesco's partners (for example; £2.50 can be boosted to £10 for use at Pizza Express). You can also 'boost' in store at Tesco by doubling up your vouchers (minimum of £5) and choosing which department you wish to use them in.

It is worth signing up for a Tesco Clubcard as they do have quite a range of offers for everyone, such as Christmas Savers, Baby Club, Competitions and Fuel Save (for every £50 spent at Tesco within a month, you can get 2p off a litre of fuel. Maximum of 20p per litre can be redeemed in one go). They even have an app (for iOS and Android).

You can even earn extra Clubcard points if you use your own bags. You will be given 1 point per bag used.

Tesco also has Tesco Bank* and Tesco Bank Home Insurance*. If you have a Tesco Clubcard and take out a Current Account, Mortgage or Home Insurance with them, you can earn Clubcard points here too.

2. **My John Lewis** – www.johnlewis.com

Pitched as a 'membership card' to sound a little more exclusive and highbrow, if you sign up with John Lewis you will get rewards and 'surprise treats' throughout the year. You will get entered into a monthly prize draw with every £1 spent. You will get previews and insider news each season to stay bang on trend. You can also get free hot drinks and cakes from their in-store restaurants at least three times a year. And you will get exclusive invitations to shopping evenings three times a year. They even have a My John Lewis Nursery where they will give you advice, offers, exclusive events and ideas.

3. **Boots Advantage Card** – www.boots.com

If you love Boots, this card is for you! They give a really generous 4 points for every £1 you spend in store or online, and every point is worth 1p so the value can really go up quickly. They too have an app so you can have all your offers at your fingertips. You can also have an email sent through with latest offers. Their Parenting Club is really helpful as you can collect a whopping 10 points per £1 spent (on certain products) if you are expecting a baby, or have a child under 3 years old. They also have special offers for card holders over the age of 60.

4. **Nectar Card** – www.nectar.com

This card can be used in many stores and e-shops such as eBay, Argos, Sainsburys, Debenhams, Next, Homebase, British Gas and many more. It is one of the most versatile cards but each point collected is only now worth ½ pence meaning you need to collect 500 points to get just £2.50. This may not build up very quickly if you only buy the odd few things at Sainsburys, but if you remember to check and use it with all the other partners, and link it to your British Gas account (if you are with them), and maybe use the nectar toolbar when searching online (you get 100 points for installing it) you could end up accumulating quite a few points without even realising. I used to collect nectar points with British Gas and started getting a lot of points from them all of a sudden, then I realised that British Gas had a price hike which made me switch suppliers quite sharpish! Getting a lot of nectar points didn't mean I was going to stay with that supplier and pay through the nose!

The thing I like about my nectar card though is that I can let my points build up and redeem them as and when I want to, rather than have them changed into vouchers and sent out every few months. I like to let them build up and then use them at Christmas – I had £24 built up last Christmas, which was the turkey sorted out!

Like Tesco, you can redeem your points in store or online at face value with all the affiliated companies. And if you wish to use your nectar points with other partners, Nectar has a 'Days Out' scheme where you can use 500 points to get £3.75 off (not a great whoop) at over 100 sites across the UK, such as Pizza Express, Go Ape!, Paradise Wildlife Park and many others. There are some places where you can actually double your points value and swap 500 points for £5, places such as Madame Tussauds, Lego Land, Alton Towers, Warwick Castle (in fact, I believe they are all part of the Merlin group, so maybe best to check the Merlin Entertainments website).

5.   The Costa Coffee Club – www.costa.co.uk

You receive 5 points for every £1 spent. Each point is worth 1p, so you will need to have spent £20 to have accumulated £1 of credit. I hope you like coffee…

If you download their app (available on iOS & Android), you also get 100 bonus points – that's halfway to a free coffee! They also say that you will get exclusive rewards and offers on the app too.

6.   KFC and McDonalds

Not a loyalty card as such for these fact food stores, but, on the coffee cups, they have a 'collect stickers' scheme where you attach stickers onto a card (also attached to the cup) and get a free hot drink once you have collected 6 stickers.

7.   Avios Air Miles – www.airmiles.co.uk

This is the Air Miles loyalty scheme (Avios now owns Air Miles) where you can gain air miles to earn free flights by shopping on their online store. You need to log in with Avios, then you can click through to a store you wanted to shop with online (there are over 200 to choose from, such as Argos, Apple, John Lewis and M&S) and you can earn up to 8x Avios Air Miles for each £1 spent. Alternatively you can collect Avios at many stores such as Shell, Domino's Pizza, Halfords, Staples and Tescos. So, in order to collect Avios at Shell, you would need to link your Shell Driver's Club card to your Avios account and you will automatically collect Avios Air Miles when you fill up and swipe your Driver's Club card at a Shell service station.

There is an Avios calculator so that you can find out how far your balance will take you and what you can redeem your air miles on; either flights, hotels, car hire, experiences, Eurostar or Disney Land.

8. **IKEA Family** – www.ikea.com

If you sign up for the IKEA Family card, you will receive special prices on selected IKEA products, free coffee and special offers on meals in the restaurant, free product insurance (T&C's apply), special events, newsletters and more.

It is free and easy to join online or in store. Just swipe each time you visit in order to gain the latest offers and information.

9. **Morrisons Match and More Card**
    www.morrisons.com

A very exciting new edition to the loyalty card schemes. Launched in October 2014, this card vows to price match to Aldi, Lidl, Tesco, Sainsburys and Asda. They say that, if you would have paid less for 'comparable' groceries at any of the afore mentioned stores, you will get the difference in points, so, if something was 1p cheaper elsewhere, you will get 10 Match and More points added automatically. And if something was £1 cheaper, you will get 1,000 Match and more points. The 'And More' part of the name of the card is to do with bonus Match and More points available in store and online on certain products. You also get extra points for buying your fuel at Morrison's – every litre of fuel = 10 Match and More points (this replaces the Morrison's Miles card previously used).

As at June 2015, Morrison's have vowed to lower the prices on even more everyday products so, along with this excellent loyalty card, I think Morrison's may well be climbing the ranks to become the nation's favourite supermarket.

10. **Co-Operative Membership**
     www.co-operative.coop

With this loyalty card, you receive the usual discounts and coupons, but, as an additional surprise for users, the Co-operative splits their profit between card holders. This means that the more points you earn the more profit you can earn – definitely an incentive if you use Co-operative stores a lot. Additionally, you can help support your local community by attending membership meetings or supporting local events.

By becoming involved, spending in your local Co-operative store and always swiping your card you can take part in the democratic part of their business – and even have a say in how they are run! You just need to spend £250 in the previous financial year to be eligible to vote.

The above is just a selection of the top 10 loyalty cards – there are many more to choose from. Fortunately, with the invention of apps, you do not always have to show your card (or even carry one); you can just let the store scan your phone in order to accumulate points.

If you religiously use your cards/ apps when out and about, it is surprising how quickly the points can build up, especially when buying fuel or collecting points linked to a credit card.**

Do not go overboard when out shopping though just to build up extra points. Try to add up your shopping as you walk around (most phones have a built-in calculator now) so that you can keep track of what you are spending. An extra 200 points for buying 4x packs of yoghurts is good, but if you will not be eating all that yoghurt before it goes out of date, then it is a false economy and a waste of food! You can check out the true value of each point you have earned by using the Money Savings Expert Loyalty Checker calculator. This is not always a practical way of working – you cannot sit and calculate every single thing – but, a good way of working is to not be a slave to the loyalty schemes; make them work for you, and just make sure you use that card or app when you purchase something after careful research that it is the best value product you need at that time.

For extra point-building ideas, keep an eye out for

recycling schemes linked to loyalty cards. For example, Oxfam runs a 'Tag Your Bag' scheme in conjunction with Nectar; you will receive 100 points for signing up and registering your card, then, if you donate any items with your personal 'tag' attached, it will be tracked and you will receive 2 points per £1 when the item is sold. You can also get extra loyalty points if you recycle your old mobile phone such as with Tesco Clubcard, Nectar and Boots Advantage Card, and you can even collect points for recycling your old ink cartridges!

You can build up more loyalty points by signing up for online surveys. If you have the time, companies like Nectar Canvass give up to 120 points for successfully completed surveys, although be aware that you may not be eligible to answer all surveys offered if you do not fit the criteria. You can also get paid actual money for answering surveys (usually in the form of gift cards for Amazon, etc…) the best website to check the available ones out would be www.paidsurveysuk.com (or, www.thesurveypro.com if you are in America). Once you have signed up with any of these companies, you can start answering surveys, and then build up virtual 'points' which can then be transferred into gift cards/ vouchers (for example, at Toluna UK, if you collect 80,000 points, this can be exchanged for a £15 Amazon electronics voucher). Again, if you have the time to sit and answer surveys, this can be quite rewarding but be warned, if you click on certain companies, you may end up being bombarded with lots of unwanted phone calls from insurance companies and the like! Be 'click aware' !

*Always seek proper financial advice from an Independent Financial Advisor (you can find one from recommendations, or have a look on www.unbiased.co.uk) before committing to any Mortgage Lender or Insurance product. Your home may be repossessed if you do not keep up repayments on your mortgage.

** If you have a credit card, try to pay off the balance each month or you will have to pay interest and charges. If you are having trouble with credit card debt, always seek advice face to face or visit www.moneyadviceservice.org.uk

14 <u>TAKE ADVANTAGE OF OFFERS IN NEWSPAPERS</u>

We have all seen the offers on the front pages of newspapers; "collect tokens for free tickets for this theme park", or, "coupon for £5 off when you spend £40 at this supermarket", etc… For the cynical, these are nothing more than marketing ploys for you to part with your hard-earned cash and buy their newspaper (on a long-term basis too if you are collecting tokens). But, these can work out to be a benefit if the offer is actually attractive and helpful to you (see Chapter 15 about getting coupons from friends, family and colleagues).

I have taken part in many offers with newspapers where I have had to collect a certain amount of tokens in order to get 'free' tickets to theme parks, but, where I use public transport to get to work, I have come across many discarded copies of the newspaper I need to get that days token! You are also doing the transport company a service as, by taking the discarded newspaper away and disposing of it properly, you are helping them to keep the bus/ train clean.

As an example of how collecting tokens from a newspaper can be cost effective (if it is for something you are interested in anyway), here is a breakdown of my last trip to Alton Towers:-

An average price for a one-day ticket is approx. £45 per person, so, you would be looking at a minimum of £90 for a couple before you've even factored in petrol costs, or accommodation if you were looking to spend a couple of days away – I live 175 miles away from Alton Towers so I would be looking to spend a few days away and turn the trip into a mini stay-cation.

You usually have to collect 9 or so tokens (out of 17-20 that they usually run) from differently dated newspapers. If the weekday papers are approximately 50p each, the Saturday one is 80p each and the Sunday one is £1 each, this would cost approx. £5.30 if you had to pay for each newspaper (or less if you have found one or been gifted one or two!). Next you have to select your preferred date bands on the application form (I try to stay well clear of school holidays dates – I went to Lego Land in the school holidays once; utter chaos! A hot day full of sticky children, bins overflowing, surrounded by wasps and mile-long queues – NOT a fun day out!) And then send the application form, with the tokens attached, with a stamped Self Addressed Envelope. This will cost an extra 2x stamps (and envelopes if you need to buy them), so now, your running costs should be approx. £7.88 (£5.30 + 1x 1st Class Large Stamp: £0.95 + 1x 1st Class Stamp: £0.63 + pack envelopes: £1 = **£7.88**).

That's pretty cheap for a pair of tickets to Alton Towers! The petrol will cost a bit but there are ways to try and save on petrol costs too (see Chapter 21 for more details). You can also save money by taking your own picnic to the park rather than pay their extortionate prices for food and drink. I mentioned in Chapter 1 about saving a certain denomination of coins too – when I last went to Alton Towers, I had saved £68 in £2 coins so had enough spending money without having to worry about saving money for the day! Also, be aware that certain parks charge extra for the car park as well – Alton Towers charges £6 for the day – don't get caught out – check the website for information such as this.

As I was turning my visit to Alton Towers into a short break, I looked into things to do near Alton, Staffordshire. Trip Advisor is a good place to start, or you can Google points of interest near this destination. We ended up visiting Warhammer World in Nottingham (free entry) and Poole's Cavern! I found a lovely little B&B in Alton as our base that (at the time, a few years ago) only cost £50 per night and so had a really inexpensive 4-night break away. The B&B had a mini fridge in the room so we had plenty of room to put our picnic food away for our excursions out.

Another day out I had planned for Warwick Castle had to be cancelled. This was unfortunate as I had not visited this venue before, but, I was able to put the tickets on eBay and sell them for £20 for the pair. This still meant someone else was able to have an inexpensive day out and I had recouped the expense of collecting the tokens, paying for stamps, etc…

I have not seen these offers for a while now, but, some newspapers used to give away music albums and film DVDs. I recommend taking advantage of these offers as this can really boost your music or film collection. Likewise, another offer in one of the major newspapers was to collect Michelin tourist maps of the UK. I think I now have enough maps to cover all of the UK and are great for when we are taking road trips somewhere and want to stop off along the journey and see more of this beautiful country.

In summary, keep an eye out when you are passing the newspapers aisles – you may see something that catches your eye and could end up being a real money saver or opening up an exciting adventure!

D J Evans

15 <u>DISCOUNT CODES AND VOUCHERS</u>

According to <u>www.thisismoney.co.uk</u> the best online voucher sites are as follows:-

1. **GROUPON** – <u>www.groupon.co.uk</u>
This company has been called the fastest growing company in history (launched in 2008). This site offers 'daily deals' to its members; 50% or more off various products, services, food or drink. The first big difference between this and other normal coupons is that when you find a deal that you want, you have to 'buy' the discounted price (for example; if a burger vendor is offering a £20 meal deal for £10, you have to pay £10 upfront, before you've even visited the burger joint). In addition to this, you will only get the deal if 20 other people also click on 'buy' for the same deal – this is the 'group' element of Groupon. In order for the company in question to also benefit from offering the discount (they do have profit margins to think about!), this way of working ensures that a minimum amount of purchases is met and they are guaranteed to make a certain amount of money (for example, with the burger joint, if the discount is only for

24 hours, then they have guaranteed to make a minimum of £200 – as some people may end up spending more than the initial £10 – which may not have been guaranteed in a normal 24-hour period). Also, in order to help the company hit the target of 20 before the deal is agreed, you are encouraged to share this deal with your friends on all the social networks (such as Twitter and Facebook) – this also helps you to ensure you get the deal you want/ need.

Each Groupon deal has 2 expiry dates; the first is how long the deal is available online for purchase. Then, once purchased, the second is the date by when the deal has to be redeemed. So, if you are successful in getting you deal, don't let it expire as then it's just a useless piece of paper that has ended up costing you money when you're supposed to be saving it!

When you have the deal, you can print off the barcode, or upload the details to your smartphone for presentation when it comes to paying for the item/ service.

Make sure you check the fine print for each deal so that it is in fact a good deal for you. For example, if you have a group of work colleagues going to a specific restaurant it is a good idea to check out if you can use more than one coupon on the table. Some offers may also restrict you to only choosing from a set menu, and may not include alcohol.

This website is definitely worth checking out. It is a great place to look for deals for yourself, or even if you are looking for gift ideas (they had a lovely section for Mothers Days deals).

2. MY VOUCHER CODES
www.myvouchercodes.co.uk

This is Britain's biggest voucher site, and you are able to search for offers alphabetically, in categories such as Food & Drink, Fashion, Travel, Days Out & Attractions, etc… You can also check out special offers such as 'Secret Sales', 'Discounted Tickets' or any offers specific to an upcoming event (such as Mother's Day, Christmas, etc..) It also allows each deal to be rated which in turn raises the offer up the ratings list so you are alerted to the most popular deals available.

You can access this website online, or via an app. When you find an offer that interests you, you click on it to expand it and show the Terms and Conditions, then you can click on 'Reveal Code and Visit Site' – this shows you the code you need to enter at the checkout, and also takes you to the website in question.

This is a good site if you have the time to be able to trawl through various deals in order to get the best ones available.

3. HOT UK DEALS – www.hotukdeals.com

This website is set up like a forum, where the deals are rated in degrees of heat! (ie: a Peppa Pig bag and umbrella set at Argos for £3.99 was rated at 98 degrees!). This website is set up for people to share their latest 'finds', from emails they have received, to deals they have found in shops, to the 'Free App of the Day' on the App Store…

You can flip between All Deals, Vouchers, Freebies and you can then click on the 'Hot' or 'Cold' tabs in order to raise or lower the temperature of the offer, thus moving it up and down the ratings table – this gives it a delightful interactive feel. This is great for expert bargain hunters to be able to share their knowledge and 'finds' with the rest of the world and you know you are looking at all the latest deals as it indicates how long it has been available for.

The only problem with this website is that the deals listed are so random that unless you check the deals daily, it is hard to keep up with them all and hard to pinpoint a particular deal that you didn't need a few days ago, but perhaps you do today…! It is fun though to sift through the bargain basement of deals and, you never know, you might find the best deal in the world!

4. VOUCHER CODES – www.vouchercodes.co.uk

This is an online voucher site that gives you voucher codes, 2-for-1 restaurant vouchers, printable vouchers, deals and information on sales from over 2,500 UK retailers and restaurants, including: Tesco, Argos, Amazon, Marks & Spencer, New Look, Currys, Pizza Express, Little Chef, Harvester and many more.

You can search for a specific company by just typing it in the search box, or choose from one of the 4 links at the top of the page; either 'Top 20 Codes', 'Smart Deals' (this seems to be highly discounted offers, such as "50% off Tefal Steam Iron at Debenhams, was £40, now £20"), 'Restaurant Vouchers' or 'Categories' where you can narrow down your search considerably.

It seems very well laid out on an easy to navigate website. You can also download the app which is available on the App Store, Google Play and Windows Phone.

The only flaw I found with this is that you could only search for a company, not a specific item. So, if you were looking for a Henry Hoover, you would not be able to type this into the search box and find any retailers with a discount for this product. So, it is more helpful I guess if you are going to visit a certain company and want to see if they have any discounts available (for example, if you were going to buy Henry Hoover from Argos and wanted to know if Argos had any additional discount codes valid to sweeten the deal!).

To access these deals, some are a mixture of having to input your contact details, and some just take you straight to the website with the offer being a generic one for all to take advantage of.

5. VOUCHER SEEKER
www.voucherseeker.co.uk

This is an online voucher site along the same vein as the above ones where they claim to have '1000s' of discount codes for many top brands including; Tesco,

Boots, Debenhams, New Look, B&Q, British Airways, Vodaphone, O2 and many others.

You can type in the product you are looking for or the company in the search box in the top right corner. I typed 'iPad' and was promptly told there were 174 matching offers/ vouchers with a list of all the results below (11 pages actually). Unfortunately, there was no way of filtering the results in any way, ie: by expiry of offer, most recently offered, type of discount, etc... And the results also showed expired offers which meant a lot of sifting through pages of unnecessary gumpf.

At the top of the page there are 6x buttons to various links. The first is the 'Home' button. Then there is 'Daily Deals' which was blank when I clicked on it (12/6/14) which made me feel that perhaps they do not update the website very often. Then there is 'Latest Voucher Codes' which brings up the most recently added discount codes, again, unfortunately, they do not seem to update the offers very often as the most recent offer was dated 14/2/14!. The next button is 'Sign Up' which gives you the option to subscribe to their newsletters if you so wish, although at least your inbox won't be filled up with endless newsletters as not much seems to be happening on there at the moment. The next button 'Help' explains what voucher codes are and there is a helpful screen shot of where you would enter the promotional codes on any given website during the checkout process. The last button is called 'Blog' and it gives you quite a vast array of blog posts with an option of sub-menus to narrow down the topics to: 'Fashion', 'Electronics', 'Travel', 'Home and Garden', 'Finance' and 'Health and Beauty'.

Overall, an easy to navigate website that would be really good if it was updated more frequently.

The above list is in no way exhaustive, but is a sample of the most popular online discount/ voucher websites about at the moment.

Another excellent website to use to that keeps you updated on all areas of finance and saving money is www.thisismoney.co.uk. Their website is jam-packed with anything and everything you could wish to know. You can also subscribe to their weekly newsletter which I would highly recommend as it brings you the most up-to-date news in the ever-changing finance jungle. I must say that the people who work at This Is Money are tireless and they don't just let you know of updates, they are there for you as well. There is a full page of contact details and an 'Experts Section' where you can email any questions to the experts and they will do their best to help you, as well as having a page full of previously-asked scenarios. A *really* handy tool is the page of calculators! There are loads of calculators that will work out: Mortgage Affordability, Student Budgets, Pension Pot Calculator, VAT, Household Budget, and many more. Very helpful and all the content can be shared with anyone you feel would benefit via all the usual social media buttons.

Of course, no section on saving money would be complete without a mention to Mr Martin Lewis of www.moneysavingexpert.com.
This uber-busy entrepreneur is apparently the most searched-for British man on Google and his website (that was launched back in 2003) is the UK's biggest money site. There are over 14m monthly users and 9m people subscribed for 'Martin's Money Tips' email (including myself). This website really does bring you all the best deals, vouchers and information about insurance/ mortgages/ travel/ energy comparison, etc... and so much more. It is definitely worth checking out before you part with any of your money. I decided to check out 'cheap broadband deals' and the top search result brought up a no-frills, easy to understand list of what the current best deals are, followed by a breakdown of what broadband is, how it works, the different types, what to look out for,

whether you need line rental too, and if you are under contract with a company at the moment, how to haggle with your current provider! Simple and everything I need on one page. The website is easy to navigate with well-structured links and sub-menus.

If you know that you will be going to a specific place/ website/ restaurant, it is worth checking out online (using the above websites or just typing 'name-of-product discount code' into any search engine) to see if there are any offers applicable to you. I was visiting Dover Castle once so just carried out a quick check and found a nice 2-for-1 entry voucher for it. Also, if you are travelling on the train, check at the ticket office to see if they run any deals at any locations in/ around your destination. For example: the C2C train operators have a booklet called '2for1 London' which has over 150 offers of 2-for-1 deals at some of the biggest attractions, restaurants and shows in London. This booklet is full of coupons that you need to fill out, but you can pass them directly to the attraction/ restaurant or show operator and, as long as you have an accompanying valid train ticket you can save a fortune! The streets of London may not be paved with gold, but with a bit of planning you could save a mint while you are there!

As well as ensuring that you are getting the best possible value for your money on any product/ service you need, another benefit for searching for discount codes/ vouchers is that you may even come across something new to try that you might never have thought of, thus broadening your horizons even more. I once went to a restaurant called Old Orleans at Lakeside Shopping Centre, Essex, as I had been told of a special offer there and it was one of the best restaurants I had ever been to! The cocktails were awesome and the coconut shrimp was a-ma-zing. If I hadn't given it a try I would have missed out on the one of the best gastronomic experiences of my life.

A tip that I will pass on to you is to carry a basic A4 plastic wallet in your bag (this can fold down easily to fit in your bag). This is to keep all your paper vouchers in one safe place without them getting lost or screwed up. Clear this bag out regularly though as coupons only have a certain life span and you can quickly have a bag full of expired coupons which is no fun to sift through when you are at the till point. In fact, before you go into a shop, have a quick check through your coupon bag to see if you have anything relevant to that store. If yes, keep them to hand so they are ready to hand to the cashier (or use at the self-service tills) and avoid all that tutting from the queue behind you while searching for your money/ card, points card and any coupons! Honestly, I have been so embarrassed by being THAT person that I have sacrificed using a precious coupon just to get away from the evil looks! I regretted it afterwards so just remember that you do not have to rush to get out of people's way (you will never be quick enough for some impatient people) but you CAN be prepared to pass the cashier all the relevant paperwork in one flourish.

There are a lot of telecommunications providers that offer special deals to their customers ('Orange Wednesdays' does still exist even though it's now under the EE umbrella). I am with O2 and they have an app called 'Priority Moments' (available on iTunes and Google Pay). Once this app is installed on your device, open it when you are out and about. It will update to show you all the deals happening nearby (as well as online exclusive deals too) and if you see a 'moment' that you want to claim, click on it and it will bring up a code that the cashier is able to input into their till. I have claimed many random things with mine; a free dictionary from WHSmith (very useful whilst writing this book!), a free Iron Man figure from the The Entertainer, money off a pretzel from Mr Pretzel, a free coffee, a free bag of Percy Pig sweets from Marks and Spencer, a free can of de-icer from Halfords, and the list goes on… It was a bit odd handing my phone over to someone but they just scan the barcode or input the code and hand it straight back to you. The retailer does not ask you for any personal details and the offers are without any strings (as far as I have found so far) although I am yet to use the online offers.

Ask friends, family or work colleagues to pass you any unwanted coupons – or better still, have a coupon-swap area at work where you can clear out any coupons you are unlikely to use and maybe find one that is more helpful to you! I have a colleague who does her weekly shopping at Morrisons and collects the coupons for the money off fuel vouchers. She does not live near a Morrisons that has a petrol station attached to it, so she donates the coupon to me! I have saved quite a lot in fuel bills thanks to you Sue! She also passes to me any coupons for Aldi that appear in her brother's newspaper (normally '£5 off when you spend £45') and her poor brother has had a few occasions when he's opened his paper to have a big hole in one of the pages! Sorry Bruv! But thank you for your kind sacrifice!

As a word of warning though, please try not to spend unnecessarily in order to gain a small discount. Many stores have come under fire for offering discounts that are not actually that cost-effective, especially if you end up wasting money or produce. For example, if a store is offering 10p off a litre of fuel if you spend £50 on shopping with them, don't do it unless you actually *need* to spend £50 in that store, otherwise it is a false economy and you end up buying things you don't want or need, and the money spent is far more than the fuel would have cost anyway. Think along the same lines with bulk-buying items too. If they are long-lasting and you have the storage facilities then it's a good deal, but, if it's for food that may end up in the bin as it will have gone out of date before you've had a chance to eat it all then it's a bad deal. For example: that 'buy 24 yoghurts and get another 24 yoghurts for free' deal may sound amazing if you love yoghurts, but if you are the only person in your household that likes yoghurt, and you have no other yoghurt-loving friends to split them with, and the expiry date is in 4 days' time, then that's a lot of yoghurt to shovel down. And you will end up: a) hating yoghurt forever more and: b) throwing away a ton of yoghurt which was a waste of money.

A final note on discount codes and vouchers: don't be afraid to sign up to various places to receive special offers. I know it can sometimes mean trawling through and deleting maybe quite a few unwanted emails, but you will also receive some excellent offers when you least expect it, especially if you include your birth details. Last year near my birthday I was inundated with offers from loads of restaurants giving me free meals, free bottles of wine, etc.. so, I used one lot of vouchers for a family meal out, then another lot of vouchers for another meal out with my fiancé! I was spoilt with pretty much a 'birthday weekend' of feasting out but without spending a fortune. For a few minutes of deleting unwanted emails each day, they are a godsend when you are looking for something in particular, such as gift ideas, a holiday, a replacement washing machine or a day out somewhere.

16 **PAPER RECYCLING**

There are many advantages to recycling paper; from reducing greenhouse gas emissions to saving energy. But, in addition to saving the planet, you could also save yourself some money too…

If you work in an office, as I do, you are probably aghast at how much paper can get wasted on a daily basis. From that extra page of a document that gets printed out mostly blank, to cover pages of faxes that serve no purpose other than to say what the main fax is about. In my office, we have quite a strict policy on paper wastage; we are encouraged to only print emails or other documents if absolutely necessary. Any paper that is no longer needed but has no private & confidential information on it can be cut in half and bundled together with a bulldog clip to create a writing pad (this saves having to order in expensive writing pads as well). Anything that is shredded goes to be recycled as well. We also have separate recycling bins that have paper/ plastic put in them so that the cleaners do not have to separate bits of half-eaten sandwich from a finished milk carton to put in the pink recycling sacks. Envelopes can be re-used for internal mail purposes and old boxes can be used to package up any items that need to be sent elsewhere. There is also an initiative to order in this grey looking A4 paper which is recycled paper and is cheaper – this is for us to use to print out any paperwork that is not likely to be sent out to clients ('back office printing' as we call it). And we are also made to order in the cheaper versions of the printers ink cartridges as part of the economy drive, although, beware! The cheaper versions of ink cartridges are fine, but, some can leak into the printer machinery and cause damage to it, meaning that new equipment has to be ordered and is a false economy (not to mention that some machines will simply not work with the cheaper equivalents of some cartridges).

At home, you can apply the above methods to also save some money if you use a lot of paper – such as if you have children. A pad made up of unwanted scraps of paper are perfect for children to draw on, as well as really useful to write your shopping lists on (keeping lists also helps with saving money – see Chapter 2).

Being crafty with paper is also bang on trend right now as well – you can use old newspapers and even brown paper as an inexpensive way to wrap presents. Not sure about the newspaper, but using brown paper and even some string to wrap a present makes it look quite retro and interesting. This is cheaper than some expensive wrapping paper and can give the impression that you have put a lot of thought and effort into someone's gift.

Also, I am not sure why people say that wrapping paper can be so expensive. I have never spent a lot of money on wrapping paper – you can get it quite cheaply from the various £1 shops around, from markets, some supermarkets, and, when it gets near to Christmas, from the numerous pop-up Christmas shops that appear. I mean, you can get those HUGE Christmas gift bags for about £1 in those Christmas shops and they look really cool without breaking the bank! It always pays to shop around when it comes to wrapping paper, and you will probably build up quite a selection so will save even more money as some years you might not need to spend any money on wrapping paper for birthdays, Christmas, etc… Another sneaky way to save money on gift-wrapping paraphernalia is to re-use those gift bags you might be given, and also, if someone has used really expensive thick wrapping paper (or even that thick foil-type paper), you can quite easily unwrap the present without damaging the paper, and then re-use the paper yourself for wrapping other presents!

There are also very cool things you can make out of paper, with various videos on YouTube on how to do it, such as: simple paper shotgun, paper crossbow, paper aeroplanes, paper masks and cool origami items.

LUXERIES

17 **HAIR AND BEAUTY**

When on a budget, having manicures, pedicures and trips to beauty salons tend to be the first things to go, but that doesn't mean that you cannot still partake in the odd luxury every now and then…

Going to the hairdresser is one of those things I put off for as long as possible. I honestly tend to only go every six months or so, and then I really *have* to go as the split ends need sorting out and it looks a boring mess. I do not know many people that religiously go to the hairdressers every six weeks (as I am constantly told by my hairdresser to do) unless they have a fringe that needs to be kept trimmed (please don't cut your own fringes – I have tried so many times and each time is more disastrous than the last – think Dave Hill from Slade!). So, as I always had more important things to spend my money on (ie: bills) I grew my fringe out and ended up with lovely, long, lustrous hair which could be tied back or curled and was ever so practical – even though I usually have no idea what to do with it no matter the style!

I am not saying you should only get your hair cut every six months. I think every three months is OK as you do need to make sure it is kept in healthy condition. But if you drop from every six weeks to every three months, that is four times a year compared to 8-9 trips a year – that's quite a hefty saving if you tend to spend £40-£60 each trip.

If you are very brave, you can get your cut cheaply, or even free, if you allow students loose on it. My fiancé used to work at a college and the hair and beauty students were always on the lookout for people to practice on. I must admit, I only had mine cut once by a student and I was put off going back purely because it took him six hours to do it (bless him). He was so nervous that everything was in slow motion, and he wasn't particularly gentle with a brush either. I am sure he is now a fully qualified style consultant with Toni and Guy, and we all have to start somewhere, but after losing nearly a whole day I didn't go down that route again.

After I had grown my fringe out and decided long and natural was very in vogue, I got a bit bored and started wondering about having a fringe again. Then I found a genius invention called the clip-in fringe! You can pay lots of money for them but I got mine off eBay (new) for about £3.50. I could change my style without having to commit to having bangs cut in again. They come quite long and I had to trim it down (oh no, not again!) but, at least you can hang it on something in front of you to work on instead of looking in a mirror and trying to hold the scissors in a cack-handed way and slowly cutting at an incline… Also, if it's not perfect, it clips in so you can move it up or down accordingly. When not in use, it lives on the head of my stuffed owl to keep it straight – we call him Owl-ton John now, with his big, floppy ginger fringe.

Keep an eye out in local papers – local beauty parlours and hairdressers sometimes run special offers of hair and beauty products.

Hairdressers and beauty parlours have loyalty cards too! The local one I go to has a card that gives a stamp every time you have something done with a free cut when you collect ten stamps – by the time I have enough stamps though, they will have probably changed the deal!

If you tend to go to expensive big-name salons, try downsizing a bit. You are paying for the name. I am sure Rachel in the local Save-A-Cuts may be just as experienced and artistic as Mario from Vidal Sassoon. You may even be able to get Rachel to come to your home to do your hair which is usually even cheaper!

When I was younger I used to change my hair colour a lot. Being ginger I hated it at school and at college. The trouble was, being a student, I couldn't afford to get it professionally coloured all the time, so I found Wella Colour Mousse! I don't know if they are still around, but they were brilliant; gave a lovely even colour, didn't make too much mess each time I used one, and washed out quite easily so my Nan couldn't moan at me for 'ruining my lovely red hair'.

If you know someone talented who can cut hair and is willing to do it for you, you will be quid's in! If you have a pretty straightforward hairstyle (guys or girls) and are brave enough to set them loose on your hair, why not take advantage of a very enviable position.

The alternative to letting your hair grow long and easy, is to have it cut very short and easy. This look might not suit everyone though – I had mine cut very short thinking I would look like a cute elf – the reality was that I felt my face was far to round and big to pull that look off and I looked like a boy. I think I cried until it grew out...

However, if you are happy to do this, it will take quite a while to grow long again and need another cut and can be very practical in the summer months. Consider donating your cut hair to wig makers as well; your hairdresser may know of somewhere.

Keep your hair conditioned. This is important if you are leaving it a while between visits, use a lot of heated appliances on your hair, or have damaged the hair due to harsh colours and bleaches. You can get quite cheap deep-conditioners from pound stores, or you can make your own by mixing an egg white with ½ cup of mayonnaise and ½ cup of plain yoghurt. Lather it up in your hair and leave on for about 30 minutes, then rinse off well. You can do this once a week or so.

If there is a specific hair or beauty product you love, it may be worth checking out if you can get it in bulk while you are bulk buying your food – these kinds of non-perishable items can be stored away and will save money in the long run as you will not need to keep buying it every month or so at the supermarket.

Use smaller amounts of product. You only really need an amount the size of a 10p piece (or a nickel), not a whole handful.

Putting a little bit of water in the bottom of shampoo, conditioner and shower gel bottles can give you an extra one or two uses!

You don't need to wash your hair every day. Washing it every other day or so saves on shampoo & conditioner, and can also make your hair healthier. Washing every day strips the hair of its natural oils and can leave it looking dry and prone to breakage.

Instead of using expensive hair serum, use a tiny dab of baby oil.

If you have sensitive skin, the best way to remove eye makeup is by pouring milk on to a cotton ball, wiping it over your eyes, and then rinsing off with lukewarm water.

Save money on expensive body scrubs by making your own. Mix honey with brown sugar into a paste consistency then use it to buff up your skin!

Putting any old bits of soap into the bottom of a pop-sock makes a brilliant buffer and exfoliates too.

If you have a little bit of perfume left in the bottle that just won't spray out anymore, mix it into a cheap moisturiser to make a beautiful smelling moisturiser that will probably last longer than the spray…

Having a tub of inexpensive Vaseline can do a multitude of things; lip balm, rubbing on ears to help with putting earrings in, heel softener, rubbing on to a sore nose, taming eyebrows, makeup remover, protecting your skin if colouring hair, helps to remove false eyelashes, soothes dry cuticles and lubricates stuck things (like rings or screw tops, such as nail varnish lids).

If you are signed up to companies like Groupon (www.groupon.co.uk) you will always get tons of special offers for beauty deals and packages.

When I was at college, it seemed as if every weekend had a party of some sort going on, and, as I worked every weekend, I didn't always have time to get home and do hair and makeup and arrive in good time! So, and I don't know if you can do this now, I used to pop into my local Body Shop in my lunch break and get a free mini-makeover! I would invariably buy some of the products they sold (sometimes!) but it was pretty cool having my makeup professionally applied before a big party!

Some companies, like Lush and MAC will reward you for taking back empty containers by giving you free products.

Cut open any 'empty' tubes of product – you will always find more on the inside in the corners of the tube!

Don't pump mascara wands – this traps air inside the mascara and dries it out – spin the brush instead.

Mix a blob of foundation with cheap lotion to make it go further and last longer.

Apply foundation with a brush rather than a sponge as you will use less – a sponge just soaks up the product, the brush will honestly make it go further.

Check out the pound stores – you will be surprised how many named brands are stocked there.

D J Evans

18 **TRAVEL**

This chapter will cover the various ways we travel – either for work or personal purposes. Holiday travel will be covered in a different chapter.

Unless you absolutely have to use the trains to get to work (ie: commuting into London from another county), or have to use a car as part of your job (in which case you should be able to claim back mileage costs) I would recommend using a bus or walking instead. Using the bus saves on fuel, parking fees, running costs of a car and reduces your carbon footprint. It can be a bit of a nightmare if your bus route coincides with the school run, as you will have to contend with screeching, whooping children first thing in the morning (although not after work if you finish at 5pm as the little darlings have long finished their school day by then) and this can be grating on a Monday morning, but, if money is a factor then it is a small price to pay, and, don't forget, they *do* get 13 weeks' holiday each year so you have a break from them quite often.

Try to buy monthly or annual tickets as this will work out cheaper than daily fares. Sometimes, buying an annual ticket can save you the equivalent of a months' fare.

Try and incorporate walking into your daily commute. If you can walk the whole way to your destination, even better. It is the ultimate way to save money; you will feel better and get fit in the process.

If a group of you need to travel to a destination on public transport, look out for special offers, usually called 'Group Save'. They tend to work along the lines of; if there are 3-9 of you travelling to and from the same destination together, you can save approximately a third of the price that it would have cost if you had bought your tickets individually. You will need to check when you can use these tickets though as some companies only let you use them at off-peak times. Also check out if the public transport company in question runs special offers for local attractions. For example; my local train network (C2C) shuttles between London and Southend on Sea (Essex) and runs a scheme called 'London 2FOR1 Offers'. They have a huge variety of top London attractions where you can get 2-for-1 entry if you complete a voucher and show them valid travel cards.

Participate in a carpool scheme with work colleagues, friends or family. This is a great way to offset fuel costs, reduces traffic congestion, carbon emissions and the need for parking spaces. If more than one of you has a car, you can swap who does the driving, also reducing stress on the one person who may end up doing all the driving. If you are really interested in doing this and want to take it one stage further, check out www.carpooling.co.uk which is the largest car sharing network in the UK and Europe. You can put in your start address, destination address and date of intended travel, and then find out who is going your way at that time. The website users have ratings against their profiles so you can find out if they are serial killers beforehand, and you can offer up empty seats in your car if you are driving somewhere yourself.

You can request women-only lifts, and, if your travel departure/ destination/ date doesn't match anyone already on the site, you can create an email reminder when any updates occur, and add a request to let other drivers find you.

Apart from the obvious dangers of getting into a strangers' car (make sure a friend or relative knows who you are with and an ETA so they can start panicking accordingly when you are late), also be aware of carpooling with kids play groups. There may be times when your child will be taken with a group of his/ her friends for a play date somewhere which is great for giving you a break, but do make sure you provide your child's car seat or booster seat, and, if you are the driver, make sure you have all the contact details of the children's parents, and ensure you drive safely as you are responsible for the safety of everyone in your car.

Get on your bike! If you don't want to drive, get a train, bus or walk, you can always cycle to your destination. If you are travelling to work on your bike, there is even a national tax break scheme called Cycle Scheme (www.cyclescheme.co.uk). If your employer is signed up for this scheme, you can choose a bike (or accessory package if you already have a bike), hire it for an agreed length of time, then buy it outright when the Hire Agreement ends for a small extra fee; if the package was less than £500, you would pay 3% (maximum of £15), and if it was over £500, you would pay 7% (maximum of £70 on a £1,000 package). The calculation is that you would end up with a bike package that ends up costing you 25% less than the retail value by getting it through this scheme.

19 **HOLIDAYS**

There are so many ways to find cheap holidays it makes your head spin! It can be very time consuming as well. The last holiday we went on, we picked up loads of brochures, found potential destinations we liked, pulled out the pages, spread them out all over the floor, made a list of the pros and cons of each place, then checked out the best deals online for each destination before we had even made a decision as to where we wanted to visit! It took most of the weekend, and we did get a really good deal, but we needed the holiday to recuperate after all that palaver. For this reason, this chapter will not focus on *where* to find and book holidays, but the associated extra costs and pitfalls to avoid.

There are two kinds of holiday: the package holiday or independent traveller. The package holiday is where the whole thing is usually arranged by a tour operator, including accommodation and flights. If you organise the holiday yourself and book flights, accommodation and trips separately, this is known as independent travel.

The most important thing to remember when booking holidays yourself, is to make sure your holiday is protected in case something goes wrong (if the hotel falls down or the company goes bust). There are three main schemes in place to protect you if you have booked a holiday through a tour operator or travel agent:

Association of British Travel Agents (ABTA) – abta.com

Founded in 1950, their members have to adhere to a strict Code of Conduct, which governs areas such as accurate advertising, fair terms of trading, changes to bookings and managing customer complaints. If something goes wrong, the holiday is protected financially so you can carry on with your holiday, or get your money back.

Association of Independent Tour Operators (AITO) – www.aito.com

They represent "more than 120 of Britain's best independent tour operators" and require all members to provide the highest customer service levels of Choice, Quality & Service. They, too, ensure full financial protection for your holiday – including accommodation-only holidays.

Air Travel Organisers' Licensing (ATOL) – www.packpeaceofmind.co.uk

This scheme protects people's flights and is managed by the Civil Aviation Authority. In the UK, if a firm sells any air travel, they are required by law to hold the ATOL licence (although not all do, so don't take it for granted that this is the case). You should look out for the logo on their website or in the travel agent store. This cover gives you peace of mind that you won't be stranded if the company goes out of business. Good practice is to download or print out the agents' ATOL certificate and take it with you on holiday.

Flight Plus – www.caa.co.uk

This is part of the ATOL regulations, but gives you cover if you have independently booked separate flights, accommodation and car hire through the same company (either booked at the same time or within a day). Again, you will need to take the ATOL certificate with you, and it should specify 'Flight-Plus' on it. This is very important if you are booking as an independent traveller. You can save an awful lot more money if you book flights, accommodation, etc... separately, and this does give you a lot more flexibility, but you will not be as well protected.

To ensure even more protection, make sure you take out **travel insurance** and have a **European Health Insurance Card.**

FUN FACT: The average cost for overseas medical treatment is **£2,040**. In the case of a coronary artery bypass and an emergency flight from the US to the UK, the total is approximately **£49,000**. (Source: **Association of British Insurers).**

Basically, you are gambling financially if you do not take out travel insurance as one in three claims on travel insurance is for medical treatment. And when you do take out travel insurance, be truthful on the application form and disclose any pre-existing medical conditions – it really is much better in the long run as, if something does go wrong, you could get stung for many thousands of pounds or not receive any treatment at all. Travel insurance generally tends to cover you for lost or stolen bags, the costs of cancelling, delaying or cutting short your trip, emergency medical expenses and Personal Liability. Be aware though that certain factors may not be covered, things such as: civil unrest, acts of terrorism, earthquakes, 'dangerous activities' (these can be covered on their own with separate insurance), visiting places that the Foreign and Commonwealth Office recommends you avoid (check the website for latest updates at www.gov.uk/foreign-travel-advice), and if you are over 65 and/ or have a pre-existing medical condition.

The best place to check out cheap travel insurance is once again from our friend Martin Lewis at Money Saving Expert. Go to:
www.moneysavingexpert.com/insurance/cheap-travel-insurance
choose which section applies to you (ie: 'couples/ families: from £30') and you will be taken to an online calculator. Ensure you have selected the options that apply to you, and it will carry out an analysis of the best deals around at the moment and show you the top 3-4. I think this site gives you more information about travel insurance than I can fit in this book!

Make sure you also have the European Health Insurance Card (EHIC) and take it with you when you travel to any European Economic Area (EEA) countries. This enables you to access the state-provided healthcare in that country at either a greatly reduced costs, or sometimes for free. THIS IS NOT AN ALTERNATIVE TO TRAVEL INSURANCE – you should still take this cover out as well.

The EHIC is free. DO NOT fall for the scam websites that try to charge you for this. You can apply for it either online (www.ehic.org.uk/Internet/startApplication.do), by telephone (0300 3301350) or by downloading the pdf application form (www.nhs.uk/NHSEngland/Healthcareabroad/EHIC/Documents/ehic-app-form.pdf), completing it and returning it to:

NHS Business Services Authority
European Health Insurance Card
EHIC applications
Bridge House
152 Pilgrim Street
Newcastle Upon Tyne
NE1 6SN

Every member of your family will need an EHIC (children under 16 will need their parent/ guardian to complete the form for them). The EHICs are valid for 5 years so you will need to check them (as you would your passport) before you book your holiday (they can take approximately 7 days to be sent to you, pending the application form having been completed correctly). You will also need to renew them if your name or address changes.

If you travel, become unwell, and realise that you have forgotten to take your card, you may be issued with a Provisional Replacement Certificate (PRC) which proves your entitlement to the EHIC. To get the PRC, you would need to call to Overseas Healthcare Team on 00 44 191 218 1999 (Mon-Fri 8am-5pm). You will need to provide your name, address, date of birth, NI or NHS number (in Scotland this is called the CHI number; in Northern Ireland it called the Health and Care Number). The PRC will be sent directly to the place of treatment.

It would be wise to save the Overseas Healthcare Team number on your mobile phone. Once again, it is: 00 44 191 218 1999.

As far as *when* to book your holiday, unless you have children, I would recommend avoiding school holiday times like the plague. On average, holidays can cost approximately 43% more during peak times such as July & August. My friend Debbie (who has 2 children) gets exasperated when wanting to go on holiday. She visited

Center Parcs one year; the holiday cost more than a thousand pounds for a week (as it was during the summer holidays) and they couldn't even enjoy a lot of the amenities or activities as they were all booked up as it was so busy – she was paying a premium price but could not even enjoy the experience as it was too packed! I understand why parents would rather pay a small fine for taking their children out of school to go on holiday as they would save possibly many hundreds of pounds. I personally find it disgusting that places take advantage of school holidays – not just July/ August but all the rest of the half-term breaks throughout the year as well – parents need to stick to budgets as much as everyone else and it is grossly unfair to put parents at a disadvantage knowing they have no choice but to shell out more. A father in Devon put a rant on his Facebook page in January 2014 on the subject, which went viral and sparked a petition calling on the government to 'cap' price rises in the school holidays. Another way to stop this profiteering would be to stagger school term dates, which would blur the lines on so-called 'peak' times (unless you have children at different schools!). To date, I cannot see that anything has changed, so, you are still best to try and shop around to find the best deals available.

Make sure to weigh and measure your bags before you travel. Each airline has its' own rules about what is allowable before they will impose charges. On average, hold luggage weight allowance is about 20kg. And carry-on baggage weights are between 5-10kg with a size allowance of approx. 50x40x20cm. A cheap way of weighing your baggage is on your bathroom scales, however, this is not always accurate unless they are digital ones so it may be worth investing in a set of luggage scales (from £1.99 at many online stores) – some of them even come with a built in tape measure.

If you need any travel accessories, try the pound shops! They are popping up everywhere now (some towns have 3 or 4). You can pick up adaptor plugs, flight socks, luggage straps and tags – even first aid kits. Don't spend extra buying at the airport, stock up beforehand.

Take a snack with you to the airport. You can even take food onto the airplane as it is only liquids that are banned. This will save a fortune as airlines like to charge quite a bit on flight foods.

Shop around for sun lotions. Again, you can even get these at certain pound shops. They will last for up to 24 months after being opened (check on the back of the bottle) so you may not even have to keep buying new bottles each year. It may be worth writing on the bottle the date it was opened as well. Just keep an eye on the UVA rating – try to go for one that is 4-5 stars. And I would recommend an SPF of 30 or higher.

Put your phone in 'airplane' mode when on holiday. This can stop any roaming charges being applied to you. You can also save being charged by using free Wi-Fi spots. You can save money on calls abroad by telling your mobile phone provider that you are going on holiday – they may have a bargain package or add-on.

If you are taking cash, change it up before you get to the airport. Rates at the airport are notoriously bad.

If you are paying by card abroad, choose to pay in that country's currency rather than in pounds as it will be cheaper for you. It may be worth getting a specialist travel credit/debit card (if using a credit card, make sure you pay off the balance each time to avoid paying the interest) as you will any cash withdrawal fees or non-sterling transaction fees. You can find out the latest most

recommended credit and debit cards on the Which? website here:
http://www.which.co.uk/home-and-garden/leisure/guides/travel-money/best-debit-and-credit-cards-for-spending-abroad/.

Don't buy expensive travel-sized toiletries, make your own. You can buy a set of travel bottles in the pound stores and just fill them with your preferred brand of toiletries. Alternatively, if you are not fussy about what lotions, shampoos or shower gels you use, don't take any with you – you are more than likely to have these supplied, as standard, by the hotel you will be staying in, and this saves you space in your baggage and stops any potential leakages.

There are various free/ cheap apps to help you organise your holiday. The top 50 have been compiled by Time Out and can be found here:
www.timeout.com/travel/features/1169/the-worlds-50-best-travel-apps.
Everything from planning, booking, navigating, exploring, communicating and documenting – whatever you need, there's an app for it!

If your birthday falls in the middle of a trip, it may be worth dropping hints to the hotel staff – my fiancé's birthday was during our last trip so I mentioned to the lobby manager and they placed a card and bottle of bubbly in our room! That was really sweet of them – and they even followed it up the following year by sending him a birthday card (no doubt to try and get us to go back) but it was a lovely gesture.

Make a master list of what is needed. This is something I learnt from my (future) mother-in-law and is a great way of keeping tabs of what you have already and what you need – including any medications you may need from the GP – and can re-used time and time again. This stops any running around like a headless chicken and running the risk of forgetting something important.

Top things to include would be:-

- **Passports/ EHIC**
- **Tickets**
- **Travel Insurance**
- **ATOL certificate**
- **Money/ Travellers Cheques/ Travel Credit or Debit Card**
- **Suncreams, Aftersun & Lip Balms**
- **Toothpaste/ Toothbrushes**
- **First Aid Kit**
- **Clothes & Shoes**
- **Camera & Charger**
- **Medications**
- **Brush/ Comb**
- **Travel Adapter Plug**
- **Mobile Phone & Charger**
- **Books or eBook device**
- **Makeup/ Deodorant/ Straighteners**

Remember: you don't have to pack everything – you are visiting another country, not another planet. Anything you don't have, you would be able to buy locally and maybe just as cheap as at home.

If you are travelling half board, you can save money on having to buy lunches out by filling up at breakfast! This may sound gluttonous but by having a hearty breakfast, this may see you through until dinner. Also (and some accommodations may frown on this) you may be able to keep back some bread and fruit for later in the day as a snack.

Get a phrase book for cheap or free. It is very enjoyable learning another language (not to mention adding another string to your bow) so why not invest some time into learning some phrases in the language of the country you are visiting. When visiting Spain a few years ago, I picked up a basic CD and phrase book together for 99p on eBay. I then downloaded the CD onto my iPod and spent the months leading up to the holiday trying to learn the language on my daily commute to work. This came in very handy and, although most people will speak English wherever you visit in the world, it seems a bit arrogant to rely on that. The locals seem to appreciate it when you make an effort in their country, and why not try? There's a real sense of achievement when your order for two beers doesn't come back as a toasted ham sandwich!

20 **<u>LEARN FOR LESS</u>**

One of the most important things I have learnt in life is to NEVER STOP LEARNING. If you think learning ends when you finish school, you are mistaken. As a species, we need to constantly learn and evolve in order to survive. And with the fast-paced world we live in now, we need to update our knowledge and expand our horizons if we are to keep ahead of the game in work or at home – this is especially important if you have children as you MUST educate yourself about the technology they will be exposed to in order to protect them from online grooming, bullying or other criminal activity.

Successful people are constantly learning. They have to in order to run successful businesses, manage their money or maintain their household for when they are out making millions! Learning about nutrition helps you take charge of what you are putting in your body. If you are a sporty person, learning about this field can help you physically and emotionally. If you want to learn more about technology, taking a course in a particular field will help with that, and maybe even answer some of the 'why' questions as well as the 'how' ones.

I have undertaken many courses. Some for free, some

for a vastly reduced price. I do these as I am a naturally inquisitive person and like to learn the theory behind certain areas, as well as how to apply this knowledge practically in the real world – for work and personal use. To date, in addition to my GCSEs and A Levels, for higher education I have completed: a Diploma in Entrepreneurial Studies, a Foundation Diploma in Digital Online Marketing, Level 2 certificates (equivalent to a GCSE) in Business & Administration, Use of IT, Occupational Health & Safety and Equality & Diversity. When I wanted to learn about starting my own business online and how to set up a website, I did not want to (actually, I could not afford to) pay someone else hundreds of pounds to do it for me when I could learn and do it myself. I had already joined Groupon (see chapter 15) and they generally send out offers for very cheap online courses, so, I read through them and came across the Foundation Diploma in Digital Online Marketing for £39 through The Shaw Academy (www.shawacademy.com). I signed up for this, and was offered the Diploma in Entrepreneurial Studies as well, for free! It may have taken a while, but I now have priceless knowledge that helped me to learn how to be an entrepreneur, build my own online retail store (**creationnationstore.co.uk**) and how to do things such as build up its rankings on Google (search engine optimisation) and successfully work with other partners (affiliate marketing) – things I would never have known about if I had just gone off and bought a website!

Be aware that you may have the 'hard sell' from these companies once you are about halfway through them. The companies will want you to sign up for their 'advanced' courses and will try and tempt you with heavily discounted packages, knowing that you will probably be interested as you have already invested a lot of time already. Do not feel you have to sign up for further courses if you do not need to. While I was doing my Digital Online Marketing Course, it was mainly attending webinars and, about halfway through, the lecturer started on about the next 'Advanced Diploma in Digital Online Marketing' and how we MUST sign up for it for a special price of 'only' £800! I did not want to go that far ahead yet; I merely wanted to learn the basics for now so did not sign up, although I was made to feel that I was missing out if I didn't. This particular lecturer was very brash and even said "how dare you think you know enough to go out and successfully run an online business, you know barely anything right now, you need me and this further course if you have a hope of being successful" !! I was not impressed. In fact, even if I was about to sign up, by that point I was turned off by his arrogance and would have gone elsewhere anyway. Needless to say, you can just ignore their attempts to sign you up for more courses if you do not want to do them right now. It is your right and you will still receive the full course that you signed up for - they are obligated to fulfil their contract with you and deliver a fully accredited course. This means, as long as they offer approved programmes, the content and structure of their courses must have been independently reviewed and approved by nationally recognised accrediting organisations (check the 'About Us' section of the website running the course to see if they say they are running 'accredited' courses).

Here is a selection of companies that offer free or greatly discounted courses. Please be aware that I am not paid to endorse these companies, and this is not an exhaustive list, they are merely the most popular ones online at the time of writing:-

GROUPON – www.groupon.co.uk

I have given most of the information about this in chapter 15, but once you have signed up with them, you will have access to the full range of online learning courses available, such as Sage Accounting Course (at Learn Direct) reduced from £324 to £59. Or a Nutritional

Therapist Course (from the Health Sciences Academy) reduced from £589 to £59.

It appears that the full prices for these courses are a highly inflated cost that they charge people who go directly through the main websites – if you see a course you fancy the look of, it is always worth researching if it is available cheaper elsewhere. Online learning (or 'distance learning') is big money as you can earn quite a good salary if you are qualified in a particular sector, but, they do seem to offer these courses at a greatly reduced rate, possibly in order to fill their classrooms up if a particular course is not selling very well.

Learn Direct – www.learndirect.com

They are "the UK's largest provider of skills, training and employment services" and offer many courses if you are looking to refresh your skills, learn new skills for personal reasons, or need help with finding employment.

They offer free courses in Maths, IT & English to update your everyday skills, as well as beginner/introductory courses in areas such as Accounting, Languages, Business and many more.

If you are looking for employment, it is definitely worth checking out their section on Apprenticeships. There is a range of different sectors such as Childcare, Dental Nursing, Retail and Business Admin. You will achieve a Level 1, 2 or 3 qualification and can be placed by Learn Direct in a company to 'earn while you learn'.

Vision2Learn – www.vision2learn.com

Owned by the company Creating Careers, they state that they are "the UK's leading company developing and supplying accredited e-learning to the Further Education sector through its vision2learn brand".

They can work with employers and colleges to deliver their courses and you can sign up as an independent learner to one of their many free courses such as: Essential

IT Skills, Customer Service, Business & Administration, Nutrition & Health and Working in the Health Sector.

Open Learn from The Open University
www.open.edu/openlearn/free-courses

The Open University opened its doors in 1971 and, as at 2013, has over 200,000 students learning with them at any one time.

As you would expect from one of the top 5 universities in the UK for student satisfaction, they have a *huge* range of free courses available, anything from Art in Renaissance Venice to Plate Tectonics to Beginners Chinese! Definitely worth a look.

Reed – www.reed.co.uk/courses/free

Yes, Reed, the job site! They have branched out and now offer a range of classroom based, online or distance learning courses.

At the time of writing, they have 34 courses available (provided by companies such as vision2learn and others) – 14 are classroom based (if you like your learning to be in the traditional face to face setting), 19 are online/ distance learning courses.

They do advise that eligibility for each course varies, so it is best to contact the course provider for full terms and conditions.

Future Learn – www.futurelearn.com

They are a private company wholly owned by The Open University, they launched their first courses in September 2013, and, to date, over 1.7 million people have joined them.

You can explore 14 different categories of free courses. There are usually 10+ courses available within each category at any one time which tells you the date that the course starts, how long it will take to complete, how much study time per week is required, and what kind of certificate you will receive at the end.

ALISON – alison.com

ALISON is a "five million-strong, global online learning community", founded in Galway, Ireland in 2007. They offer courses in 200 countries, and won the World Summit for Education Award in 2013.

As with Future Learn, you choose from 12 categories, and then look at the range of courses therein (there are 57 courses under 'Health Literacy' alone and 122 courses under 'Business & Enterprise Skills!)

The above is just a sample of what is available. You can probably also find courses with your local council who would be signed up with the Skills for Life national strategy. This was launched in 2001 and aims to improve adult literacy, language and numeracy skills.

If you are looking for employment, your local job centre may be of great help with sorting out undertaking some courses. They may not be very forthcoming in giving you details, unless you have been made redundant, so it is worth being proactive and asking about any courses.

MISCELLANEOUS

21 <u>**MISCELLANEOUS**</u>

I think I have covered a multitude of specific areas to try and help with everyday savings. Here are a few miscellaneous ones that just needed to be added into a random chapter!

<u>Smoking</u>

Try to quit. This will save you a fortune. In the UK, if the average cost of a packet of cigarettes is approximately £8-£8.50 and you smoke ten a day, you are spending an average of £1,500 a year.

There is a lot of support out there for if you want to quit. Try one of the following websites or helplines:-

www.nhs.uk/smokefree - Tel: 0800 169 0 169 (Mon-Fri: 9am-8pm, Sat-Sun: 11am-5pm)

www.quit.org.uk Wales: 0800 169 0 169, Scotland: 0800 84 84 84,

Northern Ireland: 0808 812 8008, Isle of Man: 01624 642 404, UK: 0800 00 22 00 (Mon-Fri: 9am-8pm, Sat-Sun: 10am-6pm)

www.readytostopsmoking.org.uk Tel: 0800 3 247 111
smokefree.gov (USA)
www.quitnow.gov.au (Australia)

www.icanquit.com.au/further-resources/quitline
(Australia)

Disposable Income

When you get paid, and have paid the bills, divide what is left by four weeks – this is what you have left to last you until next pay day.

Don't feel you have to spend it all though! In fact, if you have a little left over each month, maybe try and put it into a savings pot or account.

Try and only carry that weeks' money with you, this will stop you being tempted to use the next weeks' cash as well. Hide the rest somewhere indoors.

Garden

Break up and save pieces of polystyrene. They can be put in the bottom of garden pots to help with drainage.

Gardening is a great form of exercise – save money on gyms by digging in the garden.

Another use for Vaseline: rub some around the rims of plant pots to keep slugs away – cheaper than expensive slug repellent products.

Make your own compost from kitchen scraps, grass cuttings and cardboard.

Save empty egg cartons and fruit punnets and use them to plant seedlings in.

Buy garden items (furniture, tools, barbecues, etc…) out of season and when the sales are on.

Hobbies

Some hobbies can be expensive, but you can turn your hobby into a money-making enterprise (especially crafty hobbies) and also think of the presents you can make. I was learning to knit the other year and knew a few people due to have babies. I combined the two and learnt to knit by making a few quite basic blankets. These looked quite sweet with a few motifs stitched on but they seemed to be really appreciated by the recipients (the parents, not sure if the babies really cared!) as they had that little bit more effort put into them rather than just buying something off a shelf.

See if your hobby could be something that could make a little extra money by selling it online.

You could drop heavy hints about a hobby you are interested in (or already do) and this will give loved ones a helpful list of things to buy for birthdays and Christmas. A hobby such as making your own beer or wine could be a double-whammy as it will also save you a fortune in buying alcohol!

Wait before buying

See if you can master the 30-day rule. This is the theory that if you can put off buying something for a month and then revisit it next month, the urge has usually worn off. This can be applied to almost anything, and sometimes the price may have even dropped after the first month or so (especially computer games).

Take lunch to work

It seems a no-brainer, but don't buy lunch out every day; take your own packed lunch.

Also, save money on buying that morning coffee/ cappuccino by taking your own travel mug on the morning commute.

Cars

Buy a used car – it will be cheaper and you will avoid the financial hit of depreciation you get when buying a new car (about 20% of the value is wiped off when you drive out of the showroom, and few are worth more than half the purchase price within three years.

Keep your tyres inflated; by keeping an eye on your tyres, you can improve the mileage you get per litre of fuel. For every 2 psi below the recommended level, you are losing 1% of fuel mileage. The average car is running 5-10 psi below the recommended level; if you keep it topped up, you are improving fuel mileage by 5%.

Wash the car yourself.

Walk where possible – don't use the car for unnecessary trips.

Plan trips in advance; this will save on fuel and time.

Avoid toll roads where possible.

Learn about your car and be able to fix simple things for yourself.

Index

C

O

P

ABOUT THE AUTHOR

D J Evans is an Essex-based author. She enjoys adventures, trying new things, singing, anything to do with IT and is currently building her own 3D printer.

She lives with her partner and fellow author; Nicky P Gardiner (*'The Showman And The Shade'* and *'Shades of Vengeance'*) and in her spare time can usually be found in front of a computer either editing books or undertaking some new course.

She can be found on Facebook at:
http://www.facebook.com/pages/D-J-Evans/397594850438779
And on Twitter at: http://twitter.com/NickyandDavina
You can also find her on Goodreads:
http://www.goodreads.com/author/show/14187160.D_J_Evans